Kate

Kate

STYLE PRINCESS

THE FASHION AND BEAUTY SECRETS OF BRITAIN'S MOST GLAMOROUS ROYAL

SARA CYWINSKI

JOHN BLAKE

Published by John Blake Publishing Ltd,
3 Bramber Court, 2 Bramber Road,
London W14 9PB, England

www.johnblakepublishing.co.uk

First published in hardback in 2011

ISBN: 978-1-84358-393-6

British Library Cataloguing-in-Publication Data:

A catalogue record for this book is available from the British Library.

Printed and bound in the UK by Butler, Tanner and Dennis Ltd,
Frome and London

3 5 7 9 10 8 6 4 2

Papers used by John Blake Publishing are natural,
recyclable products made from wood grown in sustainable forests.
The manufacturing processes conform to the environmental
regulations of the country of origin.

Every attempt has been made to contact the relevant copyright-holders,
but some were unobtainable. We would be grateful if the
appropriate people could contact us.

CONTENTS

Introduction

KATE

Nobody stands out from the crowd quite like a princess. Ever since she stepped out of the shadows and onto the world stage, linking arms with arguably the world's most eligible bachelor, Prince William, the world's attention hasn't been off Kate Middleton. Even when her relationship with William was at crisis point and they temporarily went their separate ways, the world couldn't help but sit up and take notice of Kate's every move.

Kate is loved because she is strong, independent and professional – but most importantly because she was not born into aristocracy. Her story is a true, modern-day fairytale. She is a normal girl with working-class roots and that makes her acceptance into the royal family even more remarkable. When Kate embarked on her degree at St Andrews University, she could not have foreseen that her life would change beyond all recognition. After falling in love with a man second in line to the throne little could she have known that eight years later she would be on her way to becoming a royal princess and someone who the world could look up to not just as a style icon but also as a role model to women around the world.

A STYLE PRINCESS

When a 21-year-old Kate sashayed down the catwalk for charity in a sheer dress and black underwear she could never have imagined that a few years later fashion editors around the world would be detailing her every fashion move – perhaps if she had, she might never have worn that see-through dress, which keeps coming back to haunt her! But by the time she and William announced their engagement in 2010, Kate had already been transformed into a royal fashion icon and a designer's dream. Top industry designers all clamour to dress her; the high street is awash with Kate-inspired pieces; and hairdressers are being inundated with requests for that perfectly-coiffed Kate blow-dry.

'KATE MIDDLETON HAS A WONDERFUL YOUTH-FULNESS ABOUT HOW SHE WEARS CLOTHES AND SEEMS TO EQUALLY ENJOY PUTTING ON HER JEANS FOR AN EVENING OUT WITH HER FRIENDS IN LONDON AS MUCH AS SHE DOES A WHIMSICAL FEATHERED HAT FOR A WEDDING OR A COLOURFUL LONG SATIN EVENING DRESS FOR A BLACK-TIE PARTY.'

Vogue style director Alexandra Kotur

Apart from the legendary style of the late Princess Diana, and hints of fashion genius from Zara Phillips, the royal family isn't renowned for its sense of fashion but Kate has certainly been holding her own with a combination of determined conviction and natural poise. Her addition to the royal family has certainly boosted its fashion credibility. Not only that, but with the celebrity scene awash with fakes, copycats and

glamour models, Kate is a breath of fresh air. She is exactly the kind of role model girls can look up to around the world. She is down-to-earth, healthy, classically beautiful and educated. She is the modern day, 21st century princess.

LIFE THROUGH A LENS

Every girl has once upon a time dreamed of being a princess. There's the designer clothes, the stylish shoes, the 'it' handbags, the champagne, the precious spa treatments, the luxurious blow-dries, the exquisite lunches...not to mention having your very own Prince Charming accessorising your arm! There is more to a princess's life than the clothes, the hair and the holidays – but it's also a great place to start.

See what it really takes for Kate to be the ultimate style queen. Uncover her fashion transition from student to royalty, find out what keeps her looking so trim and discover some of those well-kept beauty secrets. And if you fancy following in her footsteps, there's tips and advice on the best places to see and be seen, where to shop for the ultimate Kate look and what you should do if you ever meet the Queen. Sit back, relax and prepare to discover a real style princess!

'BEING A PRINCESS ISN'T ALL IT'S CRACKED UP TO BE.'
Diana, Princess of Wales

Style

Does Kate have style fit for a princess? Is she our new Princess Diana? Or is she more of a Princess Anne? Can she survive the fashion rollercoaster?

Since she first stepped out in that black bandeau bra and knickers, covered only by a sheer lace dress, Kate has had her fashion choices keenly watched by millions – and picked apart at the seams by others. The fashion world and those who follow it have never been into royal fashion as much as they right now.

From polo matches and royal weddings to working at Jigsaw and nights out on the town, Kate has managed to pull off a variety of different looks while always remaining discreetly stylish. Her transition from student to princess hasn't always been easy, or without criticism, but mostly Kate has been a style inspiration, evolving her wardrobe from her casual student look to the elegantly regal and resolutely chic outfits she now wears as a matter of course.

Kate may look demure at first, but she can be daring too and has a real royal edge. She has swiftly become a designer's dream and the most sought-after young royal around. The fashion world has been disarmed by Kate and completely charmed by her fashion sense.

STUDENT YEARS

Kate's first foray into catwalk fashion is just about forgivable under the circumstances – it was for charity – but since then she has certainly come a long way from the young girl who was maybe a little fashion-challenged, trying to impress the royal family and a young William.

When Kate hit the limelight at the Game Fair at Blenheim Palace in 2004, her long tweed overcoat, matching skirt, smart riding boots and pinstripe shirt looked more like an attempt to be accepted by the royal family than the 21st-century chic that we have come to expect from Kate. And while her choice of outfit certainly showed off her enviable long legs, winning her a few points, it probably would have been much more suited to the Duchess of Cornwall or Princess Anne.

As a student, Kate followed the St Andrews fashion formula, which included wardrobe staples like boot-cut jeans, neutral cashmeres, tailored jackets and Ugg boots. Even without a royal on her arm, as a middle-class student Kate's look was particularly preppy and largely influenced by shops and boutiques found on the King's Road in London, giving her an air of aristocracy. In 2005 Kate was spotted wearing a typical preppy outfit at the Festival of British Eventing at Gatcombe Park. Her brown tailored jacket, crisp white shirt, stone-washed skinny jeans and brown knee-high boots, accessorised with a brown cowgirl hat, is a perfect example of Kate's student wardrobe.

But soon after graduating in 2005 Kate, in her university gown and a strikingly short skirt – bearing more leg than some would dare at their graduation – was beginning to show signs of becoming a fashion-conscious young woman and a style inspiration.

After an unpromising start in 2006, Kate the style icon emerged wearing an eye-catching vibrant red coat and black Philip Treacy hat – her outfit to watch William graduate from his military training at Sandhurst. The length of the coat suited Kate fabulously and the cut was sleek and sophisticated; it was a perfect outfit all round. It was the first time she had been seen at a

high-profile public event, attended by the monarch and senior royals, as William's guest and her outfit, as well as the occasion, certainly attracted a lot of attention.

From that moment on, Kate has rarely put a foot wrong and she has definitely raised the royal style stakes. Every time she has been seen wearing 'high street' designs, like the simple black-and-white Topshop dress she wore to work on her 25th birthday, it has sold out within days. And almost every expensive designer outfit she has worn has produced high-street copies. After Sandhurst, a 21st-century British royal icon was born.

When Kate went to watch William receive his RAF wings at RAF Cranwell she wore a classic white fitted coat with black buttons and black accessories. She has since been seen in similar designs on several other occasions, prompting a fashion frenzy for this sophisticated winter look. So it was no surprise that in that same year Kate made it into *Vanity Fair*'s list of the top ten best dressed women in the world, alongside Carla Bruni, wife of the French president Nicolas Sarkozy. And her fashion accolades have kept coming.

Kate's style credentials have won her numerous awards.

- ♛ The Daily Telegraph's Most Promising Newcomer in their list of style winners and losers 2006
- ♛ *People* magazine's best-dressed list 2007
- ♛ Eighth on *Tatler*'s annual top-ten style icon list 2007
- ♛ Richard Blackwell's ten Fabulous Fashion Independents, 2007
- ♛ *Vanity Fair*'s international best-dressed list 2008
- ♛ Monthly beauty icon in Style.com's June 2008 issue
- ♛ *People* magazine's best-dressed list 2010
- ♛ Included in *Vanity Fair*'s International Best Dressed list

COPY KATE

1. Blue sapphire ring
2. Royal blue Issa London dress
3. Reiss white Nannette dress
4. Whistles blouse
5. Topshop black-and-white dress
6. White winter double-breasted coat
7. Monochrome Temperley dress
8. White Prada bag
9. Black suede boots
10. Philip Treacy fascinators

Steal the style

Kate has a simply chic and subtly sexy look. She is known for her stellar style, amazing wardrobe and poise. The moment she steps out in the spotlight in a new outfit, tongues start wagging, the press starts reporting, fashion editors critique and the high street replicates.

♛

Kate knows exactly how to dress to enhance her body type and show off her great legs without losing her dignity. The overall effect is subtle sexiness and both women and men love it!

♛

Kate's 2007 winter white coat ensemble was adorable and timeless – so timeless in fact that she wore it again in 2010 to check out different wedding locations around London. You can stay warm and stylish like Kate in an All About Coats white double-breasted knee-length coat, priced at £159. Finish the look off with all black accessories including a pashmina scarf, leather gloves, opaque tights and ankle boots.

INSIDE KATE'S WARDROBE

No Kate style-stealing guide would be complete without a few staple wardrobe pieces.

Countryside Chic

Even if you don't hunt or shoot, you can still add some traditional countryside-inspired pieces to your wardrobe. Give them a contemporary, feminine twist to emulate Kate's country girl image. A white blouse, tasteful tweeds by William and Son or a Barbour jacket paired with tight dark denim jeans and suede boots will channel the country look without you having to invest in an atrocious granddad-green fleece and muddy Hunter wellington boots.

If you really want to turn heads like Kate, get hold of a tweed coat by Katherine Hooker like the one Kate wore to the Cheltenham races. Just make sure your hat isn't made of mink, or you will be turning heads for all the wrong reasons!

Floral Frocks

Complete your Kate summer wardrobe with a few light, floral dresses. Jigsaw and Kew are great places to shop to find the real deal. Don't forget to wear the right type of shoe to finish off your outfit – think espadrille wedge sandals or cute kitten heels.

Preppy Pieces

To look the part, a couple of preppy pieces are essential additions to your wardrobe. Think white

skinny jeans, denim skirts, polo shirts, round-neck jumpers and a matching gilet. If you can afford to splurge, invest in a small Prada bag or the latest Mulberry design to sling over your shoulder to complete the look.

Or alternatively opt for a sophisticated trench coat from Burberry, like the blue one Kate wore to the Cheltenham races, teamed with a grey dress and a pair of knee high boots. There are plenty of stylish trenches to be found on the high street if you can't afford a designer one.

Tidy Tailored Jackets

Want to really pull off Kate's style? No wardrobe is complete without an immaculately-tailored jacket. If you are lucky enough to have a teeny-tiny waist like Kate's, remember to invest in a design that is nipped in at the middle for that trademark tailored look.

A show-stopping Issa London dress

It goes without saying that if you want the definitive Kate wardrobe, you'll need to invest in a couple of Issa London dresses, like that stunning blue engagement dress or the black-and-white sequined Issa party dress that Kate's sister Pippa was seen wearing at an glamorous event! Team your dress with a tailored jacket, a pair of peep-toe heels, a small clutch and a simple necklace or pendant.

Most of Kate's style knockouts have happened at royal engagements or at wedding ceremonies. Of course, life as a royal requires outfits which are occasion-appropriate, but over the years being occasion-appropriate hasn't always meant being fashionable in the royal family. Kate, on the other hand, has been a breath of fresh air; she has always looked fashionable, on trend and innovative for a princess, making her a fully-fledged royal fashionista.

In the past, Kate has pulled out all the stops at several royal weddings, but one of the most spectacular has to be the black and aubergine ensemble she wore to the wedding of the royal couple's close friends Harry Aubrey-Fletcher and Louise Stourton in January 2011. She certainly has an eye for the unexpected. Almost outshining the bride, Kate chose to wear an outfit made up of a sleek and delicately tailored black velvet coat, with a plunging neckline, and a daring black ISSA dress with a semi-sheer bodice. The outfit was made complete with a jaunty black felt beret from Whiteley Fischer, a British hat manufacturer who has been in the millinery trade for more than 60 years, and aubergine shoes with a matching clutch bag.

Sophie Cranston, a young British designer for the fashion label Libélula, designed the coat, which cost £310. Libélula is Spanish for 'dragonfly'. Sophie has worked with Alexander McQueen and Alice Temperley and can name Emma Watson, Tamara Ecclestone and Jerry Hall as some of her loyal clients. Now she can add Kate to the list too!

Some of Kate's other spectacular moments have included the stunning royal blue dress, trademark black tailored jacket and wide-brimmed hat she wore to the wedding of Harry Meade and Rosemarie Bradford in October 2010, the simple ivory fitted jacket and black-and-white lace skirt she chose for Hugh Van Cutsem and Rose Astor's wedding, and the gold brocade silk coat and cream dress with matching feather fascinator and bag for Laura Parker Bowles' wedding.

Kate has also worn two show-stopping lilac numbers in the past, one of which featured her trademark tailored jacket and the other a long tailored patterned lilac overcoat designed by Jane Throughton, who has dressed both Jodie Kidd and Laura Bailey.

KEEPING IT IN THE FAMILY

One of Kate's biggest fashion influences has been her mother, Carole. While most mothers and daughters enjoy spending the day together shopping, not every mother and daughter come away from the shops with similar purchases!

Kate gets a lot of her good looks and sophisticated style from Carole. They both love to wear soft tailored jackets and neat coats all year round, traditional country casuals in the day and jaw dropping, vibrant gowns for the evening. Next time you want to know what Kate is going to be wearing, you had better check that Carole hasn't been seen in it first.

THE FUTURE

'SO DISCREET AND STRAIGHTFORWARD BUT
HIGHLY AWARE OF FASHION TRENDS…SHE
WILL HAVE ALL THE TIME IN THE WORLD TO
BECOME FULLY INTEGRATED INTO HER NEW
ROLE AND CHOOSE THE MOST SOPHISTICATED
AND PRECIOUS DRESSES AND OUTFITS FOR
OFFICIAL OCCASIONS.'

Giorgio Armani

'FOR THE ROYALS, APPARENTLY THE ROYAL
BLOOD IS NOT IN DEMAND ANY LONGER. BETTER
FOR THE GENERATION TO COME…SHE SEEMS
A VERY WELL-BALANCED AND A HAPPY PERSON.
SHE IS CHIC IN A WAY THE POSITION NEEDS.'

Karl Lagerfeld

Nearly a decade down the line, Kate has evolved from student to princess effortlessly. She now possesses a lot of power in the fashion industry and has the ability to make or break designers, inspire generations of women and influence fashion editors worldwide. Everyone is waiting for her next style move and, as a new addition to the royal family, Kate's style credentials are only going to get bigger and better.

ROYAL FASHION PROTOCOL

Although it's obvious Kate has taken her role as a royal seriously, and has made her transition from student to royal princess almost without a single hiccup, she will still have to watch what she wears and adapt her own personal style to accommodate the rules of royal dressing.

Colour

Even though some have crowned it the fashion saviour, and it can be found in nearly every woman's wardrobe, the Little Black Dress (LBD) will never be found hanging inside a royal closet. Royal ladies don't usually wear black unless they are in mourning. Unfortunately, it does mean we won't get to see any more of Kate in those sheer-bodice black dresses. Let's hope Kate finds a way to bend the rules! The Queen has only ever been seen wearing black at funerals, during Remembrance or in the company of the Pope. And Princess Diana only wore black on one occasion after her engagement – she never made that mistake again. Of course, once she had separated from Charles, little black dresses became her ultimate wardrobe essential!

While black is a 'no-no', bright bold colours are absolutely 'go-go' for the royals. Royal ladies usually wear brightly-coloured clothes to set them apart from the public. The only time you will see them in dowdy colours is when they are in the countryside, when they will wear the tweed outfits that are in keeping with countryside tradition.

Covering Up

Fortunately for Kate, she will never be able to repeat her biggest fashion gaffe on the catwalk, or in public, again. See-through clothes are without question ruled out of a royal wardrobe and so too are short skirts and low-cut tops. So there will be no more shots of Kate sunning herself in her bikini or partying in a short dress.

Accessories

The monarchy's diary is always full of dates that require a hat for the occasion. Kate is regularly spotted wearing different headpieces, from a casual beret to a feathery fascinator, and she will have many more opportunities to wear glamorous hats in the future. The Queen has great flair when it comes to the hat department, let's hope Kate, as the queen of style, keeps her hats simple and stylish and doesn't try to steal the Queen's limelight!

Traditionally royal women wear gloves while shaking hands with people, although it is not compulsory. Diana never wore gloves when meeting and greeting the public but the Queen is nearly always seen wearing gloves when touring and greeting the public.

Jewellery, including tiaras, necklaces and earrings, is an important accessory to many royal women. Kate will have access to some of the wonderful jewels that the monarchy has inherited. Pearls and diamonds have always been popular with the royal family so expect to see Kate wearing lots of traditional beautiful statement necklaces – but let's hope she adds her own modern twist to keep her on trend.

Fancy spending the day at the races like Kate? Because it is such a prestigious and traditional event, Ascot has set some strict rules for entry to the grounds so if you are planning a trip there, read carefully what the website has to say:

♔

Royal Enclosure Dress Code at Ascot

'Her Majesty's Representative wishes to point out that only formal day dress with a hat or substantial fascinator will be acceptable. Off the shoulder, halter neck, spaghetti straps and dresses with a strap of less than one inch and miniskirts are considered unsuitable. Midriffs must be covered and trouser suits must be full length and of matching material and colour.

'Gentlemen are required to wear either a black or grey morning dress with either plain or striped trousers, including a waistcoat, with a top hat. A gentleman may only remove his top hat within a restaurant, a private box, a private club or that facility's terrace, balcony or garden. Hats may also be removed within any enclosed external seating area within the Royal Enclosure Garden.

'Overseas visitors are welcome to wear the formal national dress of their country or Service dress.

'Ladies and Gentlemen not complying with the above dress regulations will be asked to leave.'

A WORLDWIDE ROYAL INSPIRATION

Kate isn't the only stylish princess in the royal fashion pack. Around the world there are some stunning, fashionable and intelligent princesses setting a very high standard. So if Kate is ever in doubt, she will have a choice of classy royal women to look up to and take inspiration from. In fact, she will have a lot to live up to!

Crown Princess Letizia of Spain

Name: Her Royal Highness the Princess of Asturias, Letizia Ortiz Rocasolano.

Date of Birth: 15 September 1972.

Parents: Jesus Ortiz Alvarez and Paloma Rocasolano Rodriguez. Letizia is the eldest of three sisters.

Married: His Royal Highness The Prince of Asturias, Felipe, at the Cathedral of Madrid, 22 May 2004.

Family: Two daughters – Leonor born 31 October 2005 and Sofia born 29 April 2007.

Education: Bachelor's Degree in Journalism from the Complutense University of Madrid. A Master's Degree in Audiovisual Journalism from the Institute for Studies in Audiovisual Journalism.

Work: Worked in the media as a journalist, writing for the Mexican newspaper *Siglo 21*, Austrian newspaper *La Nueva España*, *ABC* newspaper and EFE Agency. Television work has also included Bloomberg TV, newscaster, editor and reporter at CNN+ and TVE (Spanish television). She received the Larra Award, awarded by the Madrid Press Association to the most distinguished young journalist of the year.

Official Duties: Letizia began undertaking the duties of her husband

Felipe, Prince of Asturias, as soon as they were married and travelled extensively through Spain in representation of the King. They also represented Spain in other countries including, Dominican Republic, Hungary, Brazil, Japan and China.

Fashion: 'Her clothing is still elegant, but it's more contemporary, even semi-daring for a princess. She feels more comfortable with herself in the role, and her clothing reflects that.' *Montes-Fernandez, fashion editor*

Letizia was named *Vanity Fair* magazine's fifth best-dressed woman of 2008 and number two on *Vanity Fair*'s renowned Best Dressed List for 2009. She boasts a wondrous wardrobe full of designer dresses, enviable heels, gorgeous gowns, and a collection of matching accessories. For many, she became a fashion icon the moment she waltzed down the aisle five years ago in Manuel Pertegaz couture. Spanish women can definitely relate to her style. Her look is the perfect combination of Spanish high-street pieces and high-end fashion. In the past Letizia has teamed demure shift dress from the high street with designer shoes straight off the catwalk. Like Kate, she embraces bold colours and shops local, but where Kate looks to high-street shops like Topshop, Jigsaw and Whistles to liven up her royal look, Letizia turns to Spanish high-street brands like Zara, Mango and Massimo Dutti to wear with her high-end pieces

Crown Princess Mette-Marit of Norway

Name: Mette-Marit Tjessem Høiby.

Date of Birth: 19 August 1973.

Parents: Journalist Sven O. Høiby and Marit Tjessem. Mette has a sister and two older brothers.

Married: Crown Prince Haakon in Oslo Cathedral on 25 August 2001.

Family: Mr Marius Borg Høiby, Princess Ingrid Alexandra and Prince Sverre Magnus.

Education: Completed her upper secondary education at Kristiansand Katedralskole. Took the preliminary university examination at Bjørknes Privatskole and Agder University College. Mette also studied at the School of Oriental and African Studies (SOAS) in London.

Official Duties: Mette-Marit was appointed Special Representative for UNAIDS. She travelled to Nicaragua and Ukraine to address HIV/AIDS issues and has also participated in and hosted several international AIDS conferences. In Norway she participates in AIDS-related meetings, conferences and volunteer work. The Crown Princess was appointed Young Global Leader under the World Economic Forum. In addition, she is the patron of organisations such as the Norwegian Design Council, the Norwegian Red Cross, the Norwegian Council for Mental Health and the Oslo International Church Music Festival.

Leisure: Literature, film and the visual arts. Kate isn't the only sporty princess; Mette-Marit also spends a great deal of time participating in outdoor sports activities.

Fashion: The Crown Princess hasn't always had it easy in the fashion stakes and was criticised heavily by Norwegian fashionistas and fashion editors worldwide. But over time Mette-Marit has exchanged her classic, unadventurous wardrobe for closets full of glamorous clothes by Valentino, her favourite designer. After her transformation the princess has even been likened to Monaco's late Princess Grace Kelly and former American First Lady Jacqueline Kennedy.

Crown Princess Victoria of Sweden

Name: Victoria Ingrid Alice Désirée, Crown Princess of Sweden, Duchess of Västergötland.

Date of Birth: 14 July 1977.

Parents: Victoria is the eldest child of King Carl XVI Gustaf and Queen Silvia. She has two siblings, Prince Carl Philip, born on 13 May 1979 and Princess Madeleine, born on 10 June 1982. Victoria is the eldest sibling and is heir to the Swedish throne.

Married: Mr Daniel Westling, now entitled Prince Daniel, Duke of Västergötland on 19 June 2010. The wedding took place in Storkyrkan, Stockholm.

Education: Victoria is exceptionally well educated and is a very intelligent woman. From a young age she has showed an aptitude for study and for international relations, the Swedish Government, international aid work, social sciences and diplomatic studies, even partaking in work experience placements. Below are some of her most prestigious educational achievements.

Victoria studied French at the Centre International D'Études Françaises at the Université Catholique de L'Ouest in Angers, France. In 1998, she began academic studies in Political Science and History at Yale University in the USA. In 2002, she completed a study programme at SIDA, the Swedish International Development Cooperation Agency, and spent time in countries such as Uganda and Ethiopia. In 2003, she completed basic military training at SWEDINT (the Swedish Armed Forces International Centre). In June 2005, she visited Turkey with Thomas Östros, the Swedish Minister for Trade and Industry, in order to promote relations between Sweden and Turkey.

Fashion: Victoria doesn't just have a great mind; she also has a great sense of style, lucky her! Her wedding to Daniel Westling really showed

Victoria to have an eye for fashion. She looked every inch the fairytale princess in a cream coloured duchess satin gown designed for her by Par Engsheden. Not forgetting the back of the dress, Engsheden's design featured an exquisite v-shaped back and a five-metre train. Victoria's choice of jewellery included the same tiara her mother Queen Silvia had worn to her wedding in 1976. After the ceremony, the lavish celebrations continued. Just like a real-life fairytale, a beautiful open-top horse-drawn carriage carried the couple through the streets of Stockholm before arriving at the royal barge. Across the harbour at Drottningholm Palace, the happy couple continued their celebrations with friends.

Queen Rania of Jordan

Name: Her Majesty Queen Rania Al Abdullah.

Date of Birth: 31 August 1970.

Married: King Abdullah II bin Al Hussein of Jordan on 10 June 1993.

Family: Prince Hussein, Princess Iman, Princess Salma, and Prince Hashem.

Education: Business Administration degree from the American University in Cairo.

Work: After graduating Rania worked for Citibank and the later Information Technology. Her Majesty is also author of the New York Times Best Seller, The Sandwich Swap, a children's story and two other books The King's Gift and Eternal Beauty.

Royal duties: The Jordan River Foundation (JRF) is Queen Rania's NGO, which gives a helping hand to the disadvantaged in Jordan. Abroad, Queen Rania works for greater global action. In her capacity as Eminent Advocate for UNICEF and Honorary Chairperson for UNGEI, Rania campaigns for children in need. She has participated in the World Economic Forum, of which she is a Board Member. As an Arab Muslim woman, Queen Rania is also dedicated to reconciling people of different faiths and cultures.

Leisure: Rania is a keen runner and enjoys spending time with her family and friends in Aqaba. She likes to relax with a book. She also makes chocolate chip cookies.

Fashion: Rania is beautiful, vibrant and contemporary – and she's a royal fashion chameleon with a different look for every occasion. Rania relies on simple colours, such as grey, beige, black and white, especially when she's working on important campaigns. But she can also be a very glamorous Queen when she opts for flowing, glamorous gowns to undertake her royal duties.

'I JUST WAKE UP AND FEEL LIKE A REGULAR PERSON. AT THE END OF THE DAY YOU ARE LIVING YOUR LIFE FOR THE PEOPLE THAT YOU REPRESENT. IT'S AN HONOUR AND A PRIVILEGE TO HAVE THAT CHANCE TO MAKE A DIFFERENCE – A QUALITATIVE DIFFERENCE IN PEOPLE'S LIVES – AND IT'S MY RESPONSIBILITY TO MAKE THE MOST OUT OF THAT OPPORTUNITY.'

Queen Rania

Photographer Mario Testino, the British royal family's photographer of choice, loved Rania's style so much he did a shot with her for *Vanity Fair*. Queen Rania told *Elle* magazine: 'For me, I think, as with every other woman, your clothes are an expression of yourself and of how you feel, and I have found that, over the years, I've gotten comfortable with a particular style. And in my situation, also, there's the added factor that when I choose something to wear, I realise that I'm not just dressing for myself, especially when I am abroad, I'm representing my country, I'm representing my people, so I have to always make sure that, I'm representing them the best way I possibly can.'

Crown Princess Mary of Denmark

Name: Mary Elizabeth, Crown Princess, Countess of Monpezat.

Date of Birth: 5 February 1972.

Parents: Daughter of Professor John Dalgleish Donaldson and Henrietta Clark Donaldson.

Married: HRH Crown Prince Frederik at Copenhagen Cathedral.

Education: Her Royal Highness enrolled at the University of Tasmania in 1989 and graduated in 1994 with a Bachelor's degree in Commerce and Law (B Com. LLB). She obtained a Certificate in Advertising from the Advertising Federation of Australia (AFA) and a Certificate in Direct Marketing from the Australian Direct Marketing Association.

Work: After completion of her university degree, the Crown Princess moved to Melbourne to hold the position of Account Executive with the worldwide advertising agency DDB Needham. Mary's career path continued with a position as Account Manager with MOJO Partners, also in Melbourne and Account Director with the international advertising agency Young and Rubicam in Sydney. For a short period she taught English at a business school in Paris. Later in 2002 The Crown Princess moved to Denmark and was employed by Microsoft Business Solutions as a Project Consultant for business development, communications, and marketing.

Fashion: Ever since Mary married Frederik, she has covered gossip magazines in both Australia and Europe and has become a fashion celebrity. Her style is discreet, feminine, chic, and elegant. Mary demonstrates at every royal and non-royal occasion that she can be a style success in any type of ensemble.

Crown Princess Masako of Japan

Name: Crown Princess Masako of Japan.

Date of Birth: 9 December 1963.

Parents: Hisashi Owada. She has two younger sisters, twins named Setsuko and Reiko.

Married: Crown Prince Naruhito, the first son of the Emperor Akihito and the Empress Michiko on 9 June 1993.

Family: The Crown Prince and Crown Princess have one child, Princess Aiko. Her official title is *Toshi no Miya*, or Princess Toshi. She was born on 1 December 2001.

Education: Princess Masako holds a Bachelor of Arts *magna cum laude* in Economics from Harvard University.

Work: Masako was formerly employed by the Japanese Ministry of Foreign Affairs.

Fashion: Masako is rarely seen in the public eye but when she does make an appearance she looks every inch a Japanese royal princess in ultra-tailored suits or traditional kimonos.

Hair and Beauty

HAIR CARE

Kate's hair has been the envy of many modern women. Her lustrous locks enhance her natural beauty and the sparkle in her eyes. When she stepped out into the limelight for the announcement of her engagement to William, her glossy locks all but outshone the sparkly 18-carat oval sapphire ring. In comparison to the likes of Cheryl Cole and Katie Price, her voluminous, no-fuss, shiny hair was understated and every inch her own. And despite Cheryl having the 'do' of the moment, it is Kate's hairstyle that everyone is rushing to copy. A new era of replica haircuts is in full force and every girl is heading to the salon to get 'The Kate' – even Stateside.

Kate has maintained and kept her natural bouncy locks the same, day in, day out, for eight years. From the rich chestnut brown colour to the glossy, loose curls, she has definitely found her magic hair formula.

Kate owes her lovely long locks to regular trips to Chelsea hairdresser Richard Ward. She has been going to his prestigious salon for around five years for a £105 cut and blow-dry. No wonder her hair always looks in tip-top condition!

Richard Ward Salon

On his website, Richard Ward is described as an award-winning celebrity hairdresser, one of the industry's 'leading lights', and 'the media's most wanted': 'Pioneer of the "Super Salon" concept, his über-cool award-winning Sloane Square salon plays host to a team of 75 expert staff, looking after the hair and beauty needs of not only a glittering celebrity clientele but also over 1,000 clients per week.'

Hairdresser Extraordinaire

James Pryce, with his wonderful talent and creative mind, is the main man behind Kate's gorgeous hair.

James has over 15 years of experience and has worked for the likes of Trevor Sorbie and Daniel Galvin, so it's no wonder Kate chose him as her personal stylist. According to the Richard Ward website, James 'specialises in precision and designer cutting of both long and short hair; his hair philosophy is that a great look lies in the cut and his diverse technical abilities have led to him building a strong following.'

Sadly, we can't all get our hair done on a princess's budget but there

---

Who you might find at Richard Ward's Salon
❀ Tara Palmer Tomkinson
❀ Lady Isabella Hervey
❀ Lisa Snowdon

are certain tricks to the trade that will ensure that you get healthy, shiny hair just like Kate's.

Shhh! Tips to achieve royal hair

Washing

❀ Forget what you have been told; it isn't good to wash your hair every day. For the best-kept tresses, wash your hair every two to three days. Washing your hair too often strips it of its essential oils and leaves it looking dull and tired.

❀ Give your hair a treat once every two weeks by indulging in a deep conditioning mask. This will revitalise it and help replenish lost moisture.

❀ Keep away from harsh chemicals as they strip your hair of its shine – instead, opt for organic products where possible.

❀ Always towel-dry hair before conditioning it, otherwise you could be diluting the conditioner.

❀ After you have washed your hair, always do the last rinse with cold water to encourage it to shine.

Styling

❀ If you want loose, bouncy curls like Kate, don't over-style your hair. Over-styled or poker-straight hair is very unnatural. Keep your hair as close to what Mother Nature gave you as you can to keep it sexy, sassy and carefree.

❀ It has long been a staple beauty mantra – if you want healthy hair, book an appointment with your hairdresser for a trim every six to eight weeks. Not only will this get rid of your split ends but it will encourage hair growth and leave your hair looking super healthy just like Kate's.

❀ Heat and UV rays also have a huge impact on the look and feel of your hair. This means that if you enjoy holidaying in the sun or skiing in the Alps like Kate then it can be hazardous to your hair. To protect her mane from the sun's rays Kate will probably use a protection spray. Keep your mane protected too by investing in a UV and heat protection spray, or rub a small amount of sunscreen into your hair before stepping out into the sun.

❀ Natural heat isn't the only culprit for dry, damaged hair. Styling tools like hairdryers, curling tongs and straightening irons are also main offenders. Before you start blow-drying your hair into loose, flowing curls like Kate's, apply a heat protecting serum or spray. This will limit the amount of breakage and keep your hair in tip-top shape. Never turn your hairdryer on to full heat, as your hair will just become dry.

Secret Tip

For thicker, healthier hair, try eating healthier foods. Food high in protein is seriously recommended so try and squeeze into your diet as much chicken, oily fish, lentils and nuts as possible. Salmon is another great food that will help nourish the cuticles of your hair, making it thicker and stronger. It won't be long before your hair is as luscious as Kate's tresses!

Hannah Sandling, author of *The Lazy Goddess*, is a leading celebrity stylist who has worked with Dita Von Teese, Sienna Miller and Carmen Electra and has worked alongside and mingled with many fashion designers, beauticians and hair stylists – including Kate's famous hairdresser Richard Ward. She has certainly picked up some great tips along the way, including a few that will help you achieve that salon look without paying designer prices.

♕ Give your hair a real pampering session: rub a mixture of warm water, a touch of salt and two teaspoons of vinegar into it and leave for a couple of hours.

♕ Mix 1½ teaspoons of coconut oil and 1½ teaspoons of honey together and massage into the scalp and all over the hair. Leave for twenty minutes, then rinse. This will rehydrate and soften the hair.

♕ To bring dull hair back to life, mix 200g (7oz) plain yoghurt with an egg. Rub it into your scalp, leave for five minutes, then wash as normal.

♕ Dilute fresh lemon juice into a large bowl of lukewarm water and dunk your head into it. Rub the mixture into your scalp, as this stimulates hair growth. Lemon juice really enhances the colour of your hair if you are blonde – and also helps remove dandruff.

♕ To re-condition damaged hair, separate an egg and mix a tablespoon of water into the yolk. Then whisk the egg white until it stands in peaks and add it to the yolk mixture. Get in the shower, wet your hair and massage the mixture into your scalp and hair. Leave for ten minutes, then rinse with cold water.

HATS, HATS, HATS – THE ULTIMATE HAIR ACCESSORY

Even if Kate doesn't change her hairstyle much, there is one thing on her head that she embraces and changes regularly – and that's the hat! Wearing a hat is all part and parcel of being a member of the royal family and Kate has certainly showed herself to be fearless when it comes to wearing them.

It's not hard to see why Kate, sticking to strict royal protocol, has looked every inch a princess in the making whilst attending significant royal engagements with William.

'A HAT INSPIRES CONFIDENCE IN THE WEARER.'

Rachel Trevor Morgan

THE ROYAL FAMILY SETTING A PRECEDENT

'THE QUEEN WEARS HATS FOR SEVERAL REASONS. ONE, IT CONFORMS TO A STRICT ROYAL PROTOCOL. SECONDLY, IT KEEPS HER HAIR IN PLACE AND MAKES SURE SHE DOESN'T HAVE A BAD HAIR DAY. AND THIRDLY BECAUSE IT KIND OF GOES WITH THE OUTFIT.'

British fashion writer Hillary Alexander

Boy, do the royals love a hat! Kate will have looked to the likes of the Queen, Camilla and Zara Phillips for guidance on appropriate headwear that befits a member of the royal family.

The Queen

Queen Elizabeth usually wears a hat whenever she makes a public appearance and, like Kate, she has always managed to use hats to make

herself stand out from the crowd. A hat allows the Queen to be instantly visible to everyone and to be seen from all angles.

The Queen is said to take a great interest in her hats and a replica of her head is said to be kept at her milliner's workshop. Her current milliner is Rachel Trevor Morgan, who has designed hats for the Queen for several important celebrations and high-profile events including her 80th birthday, her Diamond Wedding celebrations and for the races at Ascot. Judging by the wonderful designs the Queen has showcased through the years, one can only imagine there is a small but vague brief for the milliner: it must match the outfit, it must flatter and the brim must be off her face.

If anyone is going to be a hat muse for Kate, it's going to be the Queen!

Zara

The daughter of Princess Anne, Zara Phillips, who is 11th in line to the throne, was crowned Celebrity Hat Wearer of 2008, taking the crown from Kate who had won it the previous year. The award is given annually by Luton's millinery industry and has featured Zara twice in the past five years.

On Zara's choice of past hats, Philip Wright, from the milliner Walter Wright Ltd, said 'Zara has opted for the more masculine but highly-fashionable trilby and fedora hat styles, together with some of the neat, chic, 1920s-inspired designs. But she's also gone for some fairly extravagant styles which are both fashionable and fun.'

Zara, the stylish equestrian, who favours Philip Treacy, could prove to be a positive style inspiration on Kate...and a contender for the best-dressed royal lady!

Princess Anne

Princess Anne is known more for her penny-pinching ways and fashion *faux pas* than her sense of style. In April 2009, at the monarchy's Easter service, Princess Anne stole the show with her crazy bonnet. Instead of opting for a demure, classic hat, she sported a wicker bonnet with moulded fruits and berries on the back, which she accessorised with a matching headscarf. Fashion Editor Erica Davies claimed the 'vintage' (read: old and tatty) straw monstrosity would have been 'more suitable for working in a paddy field'! And according to Davies, Princess Anne's style 'lives in a parallel universe to the royal world.'

And while perhaps true most of the time, it would appear Kate has drawn inspiration from some of Anne's less controversial hats!

CELEBRITY HAT WEARERS: LIST OF WINNERS

2005
1. Zara Phillips/Sir Elton John
2. The Duchess of Cornwall/David Beckham
3. Victoria Beckham/Boy George
4. Princess Beatrice/ Prince William
5. The Countess of Wessex/Prince Philip

2006
1. Kate Moss/Robbie Williams
2. Princess Michael of Kent/The Prince of Wales
3. Joanna Lumley/David Beckham
4. Dawn French/Sir Sean Connery
5. Baroness Thatcher/Prince Philip

2007
1. Kate Middleton/ Johnny Depp
2. Victoria Beckham/Justin Timberlake
3. Nell McAndrew/David Beckham
4. The Duchess of Cornwall/Boy George
5. Jennifer Lopez/Prince Harry

2008
1. Zara Phillips/ Brad Pitt
2. Princess Beatrice/ David Beckham
3. Paris Hilton/ Jude Law
4. Sarah Jessica Parker/ George Clooney
5. Naomi Campbell/ Prince Harry

2009
1. Carla Bruni/Hugh Jackman
2. HM the Queen/Sir Sean Connery
3. The Countess of Wessex/Daniel Day Lewis
4. Victoria Beckham/Johnny Depp
5. Madonna/Peter Andre

CASUAL HATS: KATE AND HER MUSES.

Even before the ring was on her finger, Kate certainly had the makings of a princess. For a non-royal, she had a certain *je ne sais quoi* that normally only a member of the royal family would have when it comes to pulling off a variety of different hats. Even when she was off duty, dressed in casual attire, Kate has still always managed to look like royalty. Either that or she counts Princess Zara, Princess Anne, Sarah Ferguson the Duchess of York and the Queen as her daywear muses too! From Anne's flat cap to the Queen's fur hat, Kate seems to have been inspired by them all, even when the muse hadn't always got the look right.

HATS FOR ALL OCCASIONS

Here is some fantastic advice from Audi Meyer of Fashion for Nerds and Sally McGraw of www.alreadypretty.com for determining which hats will suit your face shape. So if you want to find the perfect hat that will attract as much attention as the royal family and win you a few royal admirers, take these tips into consideration.

Choosing the right hat follows the same basic principles as choosing the right hemline, shoe style, sleeve length or anything else to do with fashion: accentuate your best features and downplay the rest. A great place to start is to figure out what your basic characteristics are, so that you can determine which characteristics you're looking for in a hat.

Angular features

If you've got angular facial features, such as a square jaw or triangular nose, then look for hats to soften and complement those lines; think sweeping or floppy brims, drapey berets and sculpted, folded or asymmetrical shapes. Also look for hats that have prominent, asymmetrical trimming, such as an elegant, curving arc of feathers.

Round faces

The idea is to elongate your face, but also to balance it. Choose tall, shallow crowns to give your face length, or try peaked, slanted or creased crowns. Brims that are wider than your face can help to achieve a sense of balance and make your face look narrower by comparison.

Hearts and diamonds

Since your chin is the narrowest point on your face, avoid wide brims as these will make it look narrower. Otherwise, pretty much any style will work well on you.

Long faces

Go with a flared, wider brim and a deep crown to widen and shorten the face. Cloches are a good choice for you, especially if they have a wider brim.

Square faces

Elongate your face by choosing a hat that sits high on your forehead. Soft berets worn all the way up at the hairline and tilted off to one side look great on you, as do rounded bowler hats with rolled narrow brims.

THE MAKE-UP

Kate is always occasion-appropriate. Whether it's pristine and perfect for the cameras, minimalistic for the daytime or classically sexy for the evening, she always radiates glamour and elegance. With her enviable glowing, clear skin, rosy cheeks and luscious, glossy hair, it appears Kate has been blessed with good genes and requires little help in the way of make-up to emphasise her beauty.

Day Wear

Kate is young and fresh so she doesn't need to wear lots of make-up. Just like her fashion sense, Kate keeps her day make-up simple and understated.

Dewy Skin

Kate's skin radiates youth. Her good skin will no doubt be down to a combination of regular exercise to increase circulation at the top of the skin's surface, drinking plenty of water to rehydrate the pores, and a strict beauty regime consisting of regular cleansing, toning and moisturising. And probably a trip or two to her local beauty spa for a facial!

Flawless Foundation

Kate looks so natural that you would be forgiven for thinking she doesn't wear any foundation – and you would often be right. Occasionally Kate is happy to step out without any make-up on whatsoever, especially if she is going to the gym or out for a

Tip

If you decide to go make-up free, be careful what colour clothes you wear. Black will definitely drain the colour out of your face. Try to wear warm colours.

bike ride. But most of the time, Kate keeps her foundation light and sheer. She matches the colour of her foundation so well that it often gives the impression that she isn't wearing any at all. Foundation is intended to even out the skin and help cover up any problem areas like blemishes, so Kate wears foundation exactly the way it is intended to be worn. You won't catch Kate with any streaks on her face!

Rosy Cheeks

Kate's cheeks always have an enviable rosy glow. And whose cheeks wouldn't with Prince William on their arm? Kate probably enhances her glow with a soft shade of pink powder blusher, which will also highlight her lovely cheekbones.

> ♕ ♛ ♕ *Tip* ♛ ♕ ♛
>
> Forgotten your blusher? Try gently pinching your cheekbones for that rosy Kate glow.

> ♕ ♛ ♕ *Tip* ♛ ♕ ♛
>
> Hannah Sandling, fashion stylist to the stars, recommends dewy sheer foundation as a great way of evening out your skin tone. And it is perfect if you are going to be photographed at a party or another special occasion.

Sparkling Eyes

During the day, Kate keeps her eye make-up to a minimum. A few strokes of mascara are often enough to draw attention to Kate's sparkly eyes. Sometimes Kate uses a soft black/grey eye pencil to draw a light line under her bottom eyelashes and contour her round eyes. The liner instantly emphasizes and widens her eyes drawing you straight in. Kate never neglects her eyebrows, even if that means keeping them tidy by giving them a quick brush back into shape.

♔♛♔♛♔ *Tip* ♛♔♛♔♛

Treat yourself to a royal manicure at a fraction of the price!

❀ Massage Vaseline into your cuticles to soften them up.

❀ Push your cuticles away from your nails using your cuticle stick. This will instantly make your fingernails look longer.

❀ Next, file nails straight across, rounding slightly on the corners. The correct term for this shape is 'squoval' and is used by manicurists in nail bars and salons around the world. Only file in one direction for a split free manicure. Make sure you create a smooth edge otherwise your nail will snag on your clothes! A rounded shape is easier to maintain and doesn't chip as easily.

❀ Now, pick out your favourite varnish. Shake the bottle before application. When applying to your nails, only apply a few strokes of varnish per nail. After that, the varnish becomes thick and stodgy and you will have to start all over again. The best varnishes to use come with a shorter brush because they are much easier to control.

❀ If you do manage to get polish on your skin use a small brush or cotton wool stick and dip it into your remover then gently clean up any spots where the polish managed to get onto your skin.

❀ Now keep your hands placed on a flat surface for ten minutes until they are bone dry.

❀ Once dry, apply a clear, shiny topcoat, and allow nails to dry fully for a second time. Now you have that perfect 'just stepped out of the salon' look.

> 👑👑👑 *Tip* 👑👑👑
>
> **Always have a tub of hand cream close by to moisturise your skin and create a polished, healthy sheen.**

Luscious Lips

Kate keeps her lips natural and well moisturised in the daytime. A good lip balm and maybe the occasional slick of neutral lip gloss is all she needs.

Nice Nails

With that stunning diamond and sapphire ring now a permanent accessory on Kate's hand, she has to keep her nails polished and perfect. Kate is rarely spotted without manicured fingers. She keeps her nails simple and elegant to match her make-up. A French manicure or clear gloss is the most obvious choice and it's a look favoured by many other royal ladies. It's chic and runs less of a risk of chipping and drawing attention to your unpolished fingernails.

Night Wear

Kate never wears dramatic make-up even on a night out, but when she does hit the town she is a little bolder with her make-up choices and application.

Flawless Foundation

While most girls like to slap on the fake tan for a night out, the only tan you will see Kate with is a real one – or a well-disguised fake tan applied at a beauty salon. With her honeymoon to look forward to, the holidays she will get to enjoy as William's wife and the overseas royal engagements she will attend, Kate could easily maintain a year-round natural glow. But even with a tan, Kate will still match up her foundation to the colour of her skin and create that flawless look, keeping the streaks at bay.

Rosy Cheeks

For an important event or for a night out at her favourite club, Kate probably enhances her glow with a soft and creamy blush crème rather than reaching for the powder blush she uses in the day. Blush crème will illuminate her cheekbones and take her look from day to night.

Sparkling Eyes

Kate is much braver in her application of eye make-up. When it comes to her eye make-up she lets loose a little bit. Kate uses copper, gold or grey eye shadow on her lids and contours her eyes with thick black eyeliner. Her look is completed with a touch of black mascara to the upper and lower eyelashes. As with her off-duty look, Kate never neglects those stunning, noticeable, statement eyebrows. They always look every inch as perfect as the rest of her make-up.

Luscious Lips

An evening event means a touch of lip gloss in a pale shade of pink or a nude beige for Kate. But never a bold or brassy colour.

Steal the Style

Kate's Make-Up: A How-To Guide

Kate's look is nearly always easy, elegant and minimal.

♛

Skin: To create Kate's look, a glowing complexion is key. Therefore, whatever your age, keeping your skin nourished and hydrated is essential. Always take your make-up off, using a soft cleanser and eye-make-up remover, before getting into bed. This will allow your skin to breath and remove any unwanted build-up, unblocking those clogged pores which can be the cause of those dreaded spots. Try not to use any moisturiser at night so your skin has a chance to hydrate and restore itself. In the morning, apply a small amount of eye cream and moisturiser to help ward off those signs of ageing. Where possible, opt for an organic skincare range, free from parabens, irritating chemicals and alcohol, such as the Pai Skincare range.

♛

Foundation: To get the flawless Kate look, vitality is the aim. Never over-do your make-up as this will only age you. Keep your foundation and bronzer light so that they highlight and illuminate your features rather than hide them. For a subtle sheen use a mineral or organic foundation; they are great for all skin types because they contain no oils and they nourish the skin leaving you with a natural glow.

♛

Blusher: Put a touch of colour in your cheeks to achieve a natural-looking glow like Kate's. Stick to baby pinks and peach palettes for the ultimate 'English rose' look. If you don't normally wear blusher, try smiling when applying your blusher so that you can highlight the apples of the cheeks.

♛

Eyes: Keep eyes fresh and natural. Draw attention to that sparkle in your eye and add some definition by applying a touch of light brown eyeliner to the top lid and a soft black liner under the bottom eyelashes. Try not to make the liner too strong, as this will create dramatic eyes. You should keep two words in mind: subtle and elegant. Complete the look with a touch of black mascara to open the eyes and lengthen your lashes. To create an evening look, work in some eye shadow. Gold eye shadow is great for enhancing blue eyes and for green or brown eyes, a light grey eye shadow applied thinly to the lids will create a similar effect to Kate's evening look.

♛

Eyebrows: Kate has tidy, well-groomed statement eyebrows. Define your brow with an eyebrow pencil and use an eyebrow brush to keep them tidy. Opt for a pencil in the same shade as, or one shade lighter than, your hair and only define your natural shape. If you are not blessed with thick eyebrows, like Kate, don't be tempted to go outside your natural contour; just define what you have to create that elegant look.

♛

Lips: Kate's lips always look natural and perfectly moisturised. Because Kate highlights her eyes and has statement eyebrows, she never goes for statement lips as well, so stay clear of bright shades of red, orange and purple. Instead, go *au naturel* or opt for subtle browns, nudes, rosy pinks, and clear gloss to emulate her look.

A PAMPERED PRINCESS

At some time or other, every woman has dreamed of being a princess. There's the glamorous closet, the enviable skyscraper shoes, the designer handbags, the exquisite dining, the luxury spa treatments, the regular blow dries and the exclusive events. In fact, the list is endless.

Unfortunately, we don't all have a rich future King for a boyfriend, but that doesn't mean we can't indulge in a little princess pampering once in a while. Follow the itinerary below and for one day only fill your life with girly lunches, exercise, manicures, facials, blow-dries and champagne cocktails – the perfect way to spend a day living like Kate. Be prepared to become a pampered princess...

Exercise

☑ Start your day, like Kate, with a spot of gentle exercise to get your heart pumping. Simple and effective exercises include cycling, swimming and jogging. Or, for a healthy glow just like Kate's, go for a brisk early-morning walk or a quick run depending on your level of fitness.

Spa

☑ Facial. To get flawless, glowing skin like Kate's, book yourself into your local spa for a facial. Try the popular microdermabrasion facial or opt for a classic face peel, both of which will leave your skin awake and rejuvenated.

☑ Eyebrows. Kate's statement eyebrows shape her face perfectly and give her a sophisticated and polished appearance. To achieve similar results, ask your beautician to shape your eyebrows and enhance them in this way to give you a dramatic, classy look.

☑ Manicure. Nothing helps to achieve that polished look better than well-manicured nails. Go for a French polish to keep your nails neat and tidy, which will make your hands look slender and elegant. If your nails aren't your best feature you could always ask your manicurist for alternative ways to achieve this look.

☑ Massage. To take away all the tension from your shoulders and back, which can often show in your face, make sure you book in for a massage to help you unwind and give you that feelgood factor.

Lunch

☑ Eat. Head to a sushi bar for a light, healthy lunch packed full of protein and omega-3 fatty acids to keep your skin and body in tip-top condition.

☑ Drink. Indulge like a princess and allow yourself a glass of

♛♛♛ *Tip* ♛♛♛

Kate likes to shop in casual, comfy clothes. So think about wearing a pair of classic, flat ballet pumps or a pair of fashionable skinny jeans tucked into a pair of Ugg-style boots.

champagne to wash the sushi down. But don't forget to also order a bottle of water to rehydrate your skin.

Hairdresser

☑ Blow-dry. Instead of styling your hair yourself, head to your favourite salon to relax and unwind as your hairdresser gives you a perfectly-coiffed 'Kate' do.

Night Out

☑ Meet friends at a swanky nightclub or bar for a girly gossip and relax with a few classic cocktails. Who knows – you might even meet your own Prince Charming, if you don't already have one!

A Fairytale

PRINCE CHARMING

William is a modern prince and a man of his time. But every prince needs a princess, and for William this was to be Kate. Their love story is a modern-day fairytale come true – and it definitely has a happy ending.

Their story began in 2001 when William arrived at St Andrews University to embark on a four-year Geography course. His stint at St Andrews broke with 150 years of royal family tradition, but it offered him salvation and an escape from royal life. St Andrews was also to offer something else, something William could never have foreseen: unconditional love. That same year a young, down-to-earth, alluring middle-class girl arrived at St Andrews University ready to take on the challenges of university life.

> **'I JUST WANT TO GO TO UNIVERSITY AND HAVE FUN. I WANT TO GO THERE AND BE AN ORDINARY STUDENT. I MEAN, I'M ONLY GOING TO UNIVERSITY. IT'S NOT LIKE I'M GETTING MARRIED – THOUGH THAT'S WHAT IT FEELS LIKE SOMETIMES.'**
>
> *Prince William*

Left alone by the prying eyes of the media, William soon created special bonds with fellow students in his halls, Sallies. One of those residents just happened to be the beautiful brunette who wore nothing but her underwear and a sheer dress as she sashayed down the catwalk – Kate – and their two worlds couldn't have been further apart. William was of course born into vast wealth, had ancient ancestry, and had been dubbed the world's most eligible bachelor. Kate, on the other hand, was a middle-class woman with working-

class family roots, and she was unknown to the world. But that was all to change.

As it turned out, their studies and accommodation were not to be the only things the two friends had in common. Kate loved playing sports, was a keen skier and adored the countryside, just like William, and importantly they both moved in the same circles. Without any training, Kate ticked all the right boxes. The couple were destined to form a solid friendship and by their second year, they had moved into a shared Georgian house with two male friends. From this moment on their friendship soon blossomed into romance, courtship, and finally marriage. Kate is now destined to be one of the most famous women in the world.

'WE ENDED UP BEING FRIENDS FOR A WHILE AND THAT WAS A GOOD FOUNDATION BECAUSE I DO GENUINELY BELIEVE NOW THAT BEING FRIENDS WITH ONE ANOTHER IS A MASSIVE ADVANTAGE. IT JUST WENT FROM THERE AND OVER THE YEARS I KNEW THINGS WERE GETTING BETTER AND BETTER.' *Kate*

Steal the Style

Everyone remembers that famous picture of Britney Spears and her then boyfriend Justin Timberlake daring to commit not one, but two fashion crimes at the same time. The couple turned up for the 2001 American Music Awards in co-ordinated denim outfits! Other celebrities, like David and Victoria Beckham, have subtly managed to pull off successful co-ordinated outfits without looking like they have tried on each other's clothes. Sometimes subtlety in matching outfits is enough to take an outfit from ordinary to extraordinary. It's like accessorising, only better – when it is done correctly.

During their eight years together, William and Kate have successfully pulled off a few matching outfits, most notably in the countryside and at the Cheltenham horse races.

At the 2007 Cheltenham races Kate and William were pictured wearing matching tweed jackets and crisp blue shirts. The ensemble especially worked for them because they wore different colour jackets. William was in a moss green colour while Kate opted for a dull chocolate brown, but William's chocolate-coloured trousers complimented Kate's skirt and jacket. The Cheltenham festival is not like the fashion parade found at Royal Ascot; it's traditional and more understated so Kate and William's sensible outfits were fitting for the occasion. Head to Sloane Square or shop at Joules if you want to emulate their look.

ELIGIBLE BACHELORS

If you want to be a princess, you'll need to bag yourself a prince! Here's a list of the most eligible royal bachelors from around the world.

♛

Prince Harry

Now that William is officially spoken for, Harry is perhaps the number one most eligible bachelor – but you will need to tame his wild ways!

♛

Prince Philippos of Greece

In Denmark, he is officially styled His Royal Highness Prince Philippos of Greece and Denmark – even though the monarchy has been officially abolished.

♛

Sheikh Hamdan bin Mohammed bin Rashid al Maktoum of the United Arab Emirates

He is the hereditary Prince of Dubai and the second-eldest son of Sheikh Mohammed bin Rashid Al Maktoum and Sheikha Hind bint Maktoum bin Juma Al Maktoum.

♛

Andrea Casiraghi of Monaco

Andrea is the first of three children born to Caroline, Princess of Hanover and her second husband, the late Stefano Casiraghi, an heir to an Italian oil fortune. He is currently second in line to the Monégasque throne after his mother.

Prince Carl Philip of Sweden

Prince Carl is the second child of three children and only son of King Carl XVI Gustaf and Queen Silvia of Sweden. Prince Carl Philip is second in the line of succession, after his older sister, Crown Princess Victoria.

Prince Amedeo of Belgium

Amedeo is a member of the Belgian royal family and heir to the headship of the House of Austria-Este, a cadet branch of the House of Habsburg-Lorraine.

PRINCESS IN TRAINING – ETIQUETTE AND PROTOCOL

If you do manage to find yourself a real royal prince, you may need some practise learning the art of becoming a princess. Being a princess is a full-time job.

'IT IS OBVIOUSLY NERVE WRACKING BECAUSE I DON'T KNOW WHAT THE ROPES ARE AND WILLIAM OF COURSE IS USED TO IT. BUT I'M WILLING TO LEARN QUICKLY AND WORK HARD.'

Kate

Kate will have to adjust quickly to becoming a full-time princess. Not only will she have to attend royal engagements, follow strict royal protocol in public and deal with the media 24 hours a day, but she will also have to work hard and become adept at royal etiquette when around her new family. During her engagement press conference, when she was asked whether she was prepared for what was in store for her in the future as a new member of the royal family, Kate said: 'It is obviously nerve wracking because I don't know what the ropes are and William of course is use to it. But I'm willing to learn and work hard.' Wait until she sees the list of royal procedures she will have to learn!

THE QUEEN

The British royal household is one of the last few remaining examples of first-class etiquette and the royal family are defenders of upper-class protocol. There is no other establishment that prides itself so much on its traditions and their upkeep as the British royal family. Although some traditional protocols have been shelved to keep up-to-date with changes in society, many of these customs remain in practice today.

Greeting the Queen

The Queen is always addressed initially as 'Your Majesty', then as 'Ma'am'. If you are not sure how to pronounce it, Ma'am should rhyme with jam, not palm. You should also treat other members of the royal household the same; for instance a male Royal would be addressed first as 'Your Royal Highness' and then 'Sir'. Do not touch or kiss the Queen.

Recently, US President Barack Obama and his wife Michelle visited the Queen. Even when posing for a picture, they stood apart with their hands in the front of them, without touching the Queen.

Curtsy or Bow?

According to *ABC News*: 'As an American when you're actually meeting the Queen you don't have to do a curtsy or a bow, because she's not the head of the state of America'. That's true, and in fact nowadays it is no longer considered necessary to bow or curtsy to the Queen even if you are British. Nonetheless, many people still curtsy or bow when they are greeted by the Queen and the Duke of Edinburgh.

President Obama is not a subject of the royal family, so he did not need to bow when he met the British royals, but recognising British traditions and acting graciously, he chose to bow slightly from the waist as he met the Queen and Prince Philip.

And remember, just because you no longer have to curtsy it doesn't mean you can offer a handshake to members of the royal family. You should wait for them to extend their hand to you. If they do, you must remember not to shake too hard.

When in conversation

You should let royalty lead the conversation and be polite when replying. Do not ask personal questions such as 'How are William and Kate?' This is viewed as rude and is greatly frowned upon.

And never, ever turn your back on the Queen.

Royal gift-giving etiquette

Giving a gift is also part of the etiquette when meeting royalty. Often members of the public will give flowers to the Queen when she visits local towns and cities.

What to wear

When meeting the Queen it is desirable that you dress conservatively, but it is unnecessary to spend money on special clothes and hats. Just wear your Sunday best.

Afternoon tea with the Queen

Tea is usually served with small snacks such as finger sandwiches. Raise the teacup to drink, not the cup and saucer, and return the cup to the saucer after each sip.

It sounds like common sense but it's worth a reminder: close your mouth when you chew, try to chew quietly, take small bites, and do not talk with your mouth full. Oh, and one last thing – you should stop eating after the Queen takes her last bite, even if you are still hungry!

Of course, these are only a few of the things Kate will have to remember. The list is endless! But if she learns them quickly she will be well practised for when William becomes King and she becomes Queen.

♔♛♕ *Tip* ♛♕♔

TOP TIPS ON HOW TO GET OUT OF A CAR ELEGANTLY:

❀ Make sure that your knees are together at all times.
❀ Twist your body as you leave the car so that your legs swing around the outside of your seat first. This will help ensure that your legs remain together.
❀ Ask a fellow passenger – or if you are lucky enough, your chauffeur, to give you a helping hand when getting out of the car this will allow you to slide out with ease.
❀ If you are wearing a short skirt, have a pashmina or scarf with you to discreetly place over your legs as you exit the car.

PRINCESS PREP

Luckily for young girls hoping to become the next Kate, American author Jerramy Fine has set up a luxury summer camp to make becoming a princess a reality, if only for a week.

Jerramy, in her determination to become royalty, moved to London from her home in Western Colorado and spent years chasing royalty and dressing up like Princess Diana trying to attract the attention of Peter Phillips, the Queen's grandson. But she gave up her dream of becoming a Princess when she fell in love with an ordinary Englishman.

Princess Prep is the ultimate princess experience for girls aged between eight and 11. Jerramy teaches the girls that you do not become a princess simply by donning a designer gown and an expensive tiara. Grace and poise, philanthropy and strength are just as important as wearing the right clothes. The lucky girls experience the ultimate princess lifestyle and live in the prestigious Kensington area of London. Inside the school, they take daily etiquette lessons and study the lives of historical and modern-day princesses. As part of their outdoor curriculum they visit Royal Palaces, go horse riding in Hyde Park, walk the royal wedding route, and have tea at Kensington Palace.

I wonder if Kate wishes she had gone to Princess Prep when she was 11...?

Break-ups
and
Make-ups

THE BREAK-UP

'I, AT THE TIME, WASN'T VERY HAPPY ABOUT IT
BUT ACTUALLY IT MADE ME A STRONGER PERSON,
YOU FIND OUT THINGS ABOUT YOURSELF THAT
MAYBE YOU HADN'T REALISED.'
                                                    Kate

In April 2007 Kate Middleton was to become a single lady. It is thought that during a holiday in the Swiss resort of Zermatt, Prince William decided to end their relationship. Newspapers began to speculate about the reasons for the split, but according to *The Times* Clarence House made only one comment about their relationship: 'We don't comment on Prince William's personal life.'

As every woman knows, a break-up is hard to deal with, especially if you are not the one initiating it. But they are even harder to deal with when the whole world wants to know every last detail about your separation.

Instead of reaching out for the box of tissues, sappy movies and ice cream tubs, Kate ditched the break-up junk food diet and became an inspiration to women around the world, especially those who were also going through a similar experience. Despite being angry about the split, she made every effort to enjoy being a single girl in the big city, so she spent time with friends, pursued her love of sport and allowed her clothes to do the talking for her. And Kate's optimistic, carefree attitude soon attracted the attention of William, who quickly realised that he had let go of the most special person in his life.

'WHEN I FIRST MET KATE I KNEW THERE WAS
SOMETHING VERY SPECIAL ABOUT HER.'
                                        William speaking in 2010

GETTING OVER A BREAK-UP – KATE STYLE!

Respect yourself

Never blame yourself for a break-up. There is life after a big split and chances are the right person is out there looking for you. Kate showed a lot of self respect after her break-up with William. She carried on with life as normal, immersing herself in her work for fashion company Jigsaw until November 2007, when she decided she needed more time to concentrate on herself, according to Jigsaw owner Belle Robinson.

Remember that everything happens for a reason

Kate admitted during the engagement announcement that she had been angry about the separation in 2007, but she now looks back on it as a positive experience. 'You can get quite consumed by a relationship when you are younger. I really valued that time for me...although I didn't think it at the time, looking back on it', she said. So just remember, break-ups are all part of a learning curve. Turn your negative experiences into something positive that can be applied to a new relationship.

Indulge yourself

Break-ups hurt, so indulge yourself a little and do something you love – go shopping, go on a mini-holiday or treat yourself to a beauty treatment, just as Kate would have done.

Spend time with your family and friends

During Kate's time apart from William, she kept herself surrounded by well-meaning friends and family who she could trust. So just as Kate did, surround yourself with friends – the more you are able to share your feelings, the better you will be able to deal with a break-up.

Keep Active

Often after a break-up you are left with more time on your hands. Use this time to enjoy being with yourself and doing the things that you love. During her time spent away from William, Kate busied herself with one of her favourite hobbies, rowing, devoting time to training for a challenging charity rowing race. Not only did this keep her mind occupied, it also meant she lost weight, stayed in super-fit condition and raised money for a good cause.

KATE'S BREAK-UP OUTFITS

Sexy, stylish partywear

Kate had no difficulty showing William what he was missing during May and August 2007. Spotted leaving two exclusive private members' clubs in London, Kate showed she was capable of pulling off both a stylish and sexy look all at once, while doing almost the impossible – maintaining a look befitting a princess.

Kate's first outfit – classy meets vamp – came on a night out at the famous London club Boujis. Taking a sophisticated black-and-white strappy print dress, Kate managed to add a touch of sexiness to the outfit by showing off her natural, glowing tan rather than covering up her legs in black opaque tights. This teamed with a matching white Prada bag, minimalistic jewellery and contrasting big, brushed out, blow-dried hair, gave Kate a younger, edgier look then her normal well-groomed, conservative image.

While a lot of girls would try and attract their ex's attention in a statement piece – think Cheryl Cole in her barely-there frocks – Kate opted for a more demure, but still sizzling hot, outfit to get her message

---

♛ ♛ ♛ *Tip* ♛ ♛ ♛

Be careful when buying bold black-and-white graphic print dresses – on the wrong girl they can wind up looking like they are wearing you, rather than you wearing the dress. If you do pick out a party dress like Kate's print dress, make sure you have a black belt on hand in case you need to nip the dress in at the waist to give it a complete new look.

across. If any outfit was going to grab William's attention, this was going to be it. Rather than revealing too much leg in a micro mini-skirt, Kate covered up, Liz Hurley-style, in tight white skinny jeans and black knee-high boots. This paired with a soft v-neck top cleverly sculpted her petite frame and accentuated her athletic figure. And unlike the celebrities of the moment, who won't be seen in the same thing twice, Kate wasn't afraid to accessorise her outfit with her tried-and-tested favourite white Prada bag!

Independent Woman – Daywear

Instead of throwing on her break-up comfies, aware that her every move as well as her choice of outfit was going to be written about in the tabloids, Kate continued to carry off the ultimate 'I am doing fine without you' daywear look with aplomb.

While throwing herself into her work as a buyer for Jigsaw, Kate enjoyed wearing a mixture of spring floral frocks, skinny jeans in black and white, and light pastel cardigans with understated espadrille wedge sandals. She always teamed them with a variety of different pendants and dangly white earrings and her favourite small Prada bag, of course. And while nearly always sporting loose flowing curls in the evenings, during working hours Kate could often be seen with her hair tied back in a loose ponytail, emphasising her beautiful, wide smile and glowing complexion, while creating a sophisticated, independent, working woman image.

By 2007 Kate had also perfected her daywear look and knew exactly what suited her body shape. Her black-and-white spotty print dress is the perfect example. Not only did this look draw attention to her small waist and petite figure, but the knee-length hemline emphasised her long legs without showing too much flesh and the sleeveless top half drew attention away from her athletic figure, giving her a more feminine silhouette.

MAKE-UPS

'WE WENT THROUGH A FEW STUMBLING BLOCKS AS EVERY RELATIONSHIP DOES BUT WE PICKED OURSELVES UP AND CARRIED ON. FROM WHERE YOU HAVE THE ODD PROBLEM WHEN YOU ARE FIRST GETTING TO KNOW EACH OTHER THOSE HAVE ALL GONE AND IT'S JUST REALLY EASY JUST BEING WITH EACH OTHER.' *William*

By showing the world – and William – that she wouldn't let the break-up spoil her fun, Kate managed to remain dignified and independent. And it's not hard to see why William soon saw the error of his ways and eventually began wooing her back into his life.

In December 2007, their relationship was very much back on track and Prince William had soon proved himself worthy of Kate's love again. They were spotted getting cosy on a Christmas shooting trip in Windsor Great Park. The day out was William's Christmas gift from his grandmother, the Queen. It was another sure sign that Kate wasn't just thought of as any old girlfriend but as someone who was extra special to William. The pair were dressed in traditional green clothes, with Kate in dark jeans, leg warmers and a fetching brown fur hat to protect against the cold.

To keep reminding William of what he had been missing, for some time Kate still continued to party, especially at one her favourite hangouts, Boujis. But now William could be found partying with her. And with her man now back on her arm, Kate's outfits went from sophisticated-sexy to demure and conservative. Gone were the tight jeans and low-cut tops, replaced by thick opaque black tights and long-sleeved jackets, more befitting a princess-in-waiting.

ANNOUNCEMENTS, CELEBRATIONS AND INSPIRATIONS

'THE PRINCE OF WALES IS DELIGHTED TO ANNOUNCE THE ENGAGEMENT OF PRINCE WILLIAM TO MISS CATHERINE MIDDLETON.'

Clarence House

The announcement

'CAROLE AND I ARE ABSOLUTELY DELIGHTED BY TODAY'S ANNOUNCEMENT AND THRILLED AT THE PROSPECT OF A WEDDING SOMETIME NEXT YEAR. AS YOU KNOW CATHERINE AND PRINCE WILLIAM HAVE BEEN GOING OUT TOGETHER FOR QUITE A NUMBER OF YEARS WHICH HAS BEEN GREAT FOR US BECAUSE WE HAVE GOT TO KNOW WILLIAM VERY WELL. WE ALL THINK HE IS WONDERFUL AND WE ARE EXTREMELY FOND OF HIM. THEY MAKE A LOVELY COUPLE, THEY ARE GREAT FUN TO BE WITH, AND WE'VE HAD A LOT OF LAUGHS TOGETHER. WE WISH THEM EVERY HAPPINESS FOR THE FUTURE.'

Michael Middleton

The announcement when it came in was both unexpected and long-awaited. Parents, friends, people in the street, political leaders and well-wishers were delighted at the news. Asked how he felt about the announcement, Charles, on a visit to Poundbury, exclaimed to the *Guardian* newspaper: 'Thrilled, obviously, thank you. They have been practising long enough!'

> 'THE TIME IS RIGHT NOW. WE'RE BOTH VERY, VERY HAPPY AND I'M VERY GLAD THAT I HAVE DONE IT.'
> *Prince William*

> 'WE HAVE BEEN GOING OUT A LONG TIME. WE HAD SPOKEN ABOUT OUR FUTURE AND IT JUST SEEMED THE NATURAL STEP FOR BOTH OF US.'
> *Kate*

The dress

> 'WE ARE VERY THRILLED AT ISSA WITH THE NEWS AND WE WISH KATE AND WILLIAM ALL THE BEST. I'M JUST VERY HAPPY THAT KATE WEARS ISSA AND THAT SHE HAS CHOSEN TO WEAR ISSA FOR HER ENGAGEMENT. SHE IS A VERY PRETTY AND LOVELY GIRL.'
> *Daniella Issa Helayel, Vogue*

A royal star was officially created when Kate took to the international stage in a blue Issa London dress. Her look was positively regal and the beautiful gown complimented her slim figure. The dress looked as though it had been made especially for Kate, particularly because of the designer's trademark crossover detail at the front, which accentuated her tiny waist. It was the ultimate signature Kate design.

> **'I DESIGN CLOTHES FOR PEOPLE LIKE ME WHO THINK THEY'RE FAT TO HIDE PEOPLE'S DEFECTS AND ACCENTUATE THE GOOD POINTS.'**
>
> *Daniella Issa Helayel,*
> *New York Times*

Kate's elegant blue engagement dress has thrust Issa London into the fashion spotlight. The label's versatile and timeless dresses suit almost everyone so if you are pear, apple, or hourglass an Issa dress will be a great addition to your wardrobe.

Steal the Style

The occasion called for a special dress and Kate didn't disappoint. The royal blue Issa London dress, which she wore to make her debut as Prince William's fiancée, was the perfect dress for the occasion but it is also the ideal party dress for any aspiring fashionista.

The original dress, with its £385 price tag, sold out within a few hours. With a flattering design it was the perfect choice and the ideal dress to inspire replicas around the globe. Coast's 'Jessica' jersey dress, with long sleeves and a knotted detail at the waist, ticked all the right boxes and was priced at a more affordable £85 when it hit the shelves. Florence and Fred for Tesco launched a similar version of Kate's dress in store and online, only it came with a shorter hemline and an even smaller price tag. But it was the Lipsy dress which triumphed among high-street shoppers, with a reasonable price tag of £45 and a design that could have you thinking it was the real thing.

The Ring

Lady Diana Spencer chose her engagement ring from several shown to her in 1981 for her engagement to Prince Charles – and her choice at the time caused quite a stir. Instead of waiting for a ring to be custom-made, she chose a ring that anyone could buy. However, it did come with an extraordinary price tag of £28,000, or $60,000, at the time. But with an eye for style it mattered very little because the blue sapphire ring became synonymous with Diana's name. Kate's ring really is something extra special!

During their engagement interview, William said he had chosen to give Kate his mum's ring because it was his way of making sure Diana 'didn't miss out' on the day and the 'excitement'. For Kate, wearing the sapphire ring will be an everyday reminder of Diana's legacy but it will also be symbolic of William's love for her and the protection she will receive from him.

When asked about the proposal Kate didn't shatter any illusions and assured all the girls out there that the proposal was 'very romantic' and 'very personal'. But William refused to confirm whether he acted like a real Prince Charming and proposed on one knee.

British Royalty

There is a lot of history and tradition steeped in several of the British royal family's engagement rings and Kate isn't the first royal lady to receive a family heirloom.

❀ When Charles married for the second time, he presented the Duchess of Cornwall with a unique art deco style ring. The ring was said to be a family heirloom once owned by the Queen Mother. It was reportedly given to the Queen Mother in 1926 to celebrate the birth of her daughter, Queen Elizabeth. The ring features an emerald cut diamond in the centre and three diamonds alongside it.

❀ Rugby player Mike Tindall proposed to Princess Anne's daughter, Zara Phillips, at the end of 2010 with a beautiful solitaire diamond ring on a row of *pavé* set stones. What girl could refuse such a stylish ring?

❀ Prince Andrew didn't hold back ahead of his 1986 wedding to Sarah Ferguson. The Prince gave Sarah an oval ruby surrounded by ten diamonds to mark their engagement.

❀ In 1999, Sophie Rhys-Jones proudly displayed her Asprey and Garrard three-diamond engagement ring. The ring, given to her by Prince Edward. It was set in 18-carat white gold and is worth an estimated £105,000.

European Royalty

The British royal family isn't the only royal family to invest in luxury, bespoke engagement rings.

❀ Argentinean princess Maxima Zorreguieta Cerruti was given an impressive platinum-set engagement ring from Prince Willem-Alexander, Prince of Orange. The central stone was an oval orange diamond.

❀ Prince Frederik of Denmark proposed to his Australian girlfriend Mary Donaldson in 2002. He presented Mary with a striking emerald-cut diamond ring nestled between two emerald-cut ruby baguettes.

❀ In April 2009, Crown Princess Victoria announced her engagement to long-term boyfriend Daniel Westling. Her round-cut diamond ring was mounted on white gold. It was a classy, traditional choice, which oozed simplicity and suited the beautiful Princess perfectly.

❀ Marie-Chantal, the wife of Crown Prince Pavlos of Greece received a cabochon-cut sapphire and heart-shaped diamond engagement ring.

❀ Prince Joachim of Denmark asked his French girlfriend Marie Cavallier to marry him with a tricolour ring. The ruby, diamond and sapphire ring was chosen by Joachim to reflect the colours of the French flag.

❀ Felipe, Prince of Asturias, asked for the hand of Letizia Ortiz Rocasolano with a 16-diamond baguette cut ring with a white gold trim.

Steal the Style

When she stepped out into the limelight for the announcement of her engagement to William, Kate's glossy locks all but outshone that incredible sparkly 18-carat oval sapphire ring.

Kate's beautiful blow-dry made easy

What you will need:

Volumising shampoo and conditioner

Mousse or lifting product

Hairdryer

A rounded bristle brush

Shine serum or shine spray

Hairspray

- ♛ Kate's natural hairstyle is full of volume and soft movement.
- ♛ To begin, you will need to use a volumising shampoo and conditioner, which will assist in creating instant volume when the hair is dry.
- ♛ After towel drying your hair apply a small amount of lifting product to the roots of your hair. This will work well with the shampoo and conditioner to create body and volume.

- ♛ Blast your hair with a good hairdryer on a low heat to soak up some of the moisture.
- ♛ Now, using a natural-bristle brush, start blow-drying the top of your hair straight, holding it at a vertical angle as this adds lift. As you move your brush towards the ends of the hair start wrapping the hair around the brush. Hold in this position and keep the heat on it for a few seconds and then slowly tease the hair out of its hold.
- ♛ When you have done this to your entire hair, run a pea-sized amount of shine serum through your hair to add additional shine. Then spray a small amount of hairspray over the top to help the hair keep its hold.
- ♛ Now you will have the perfect Kate hairstyle without spending £150!
- ♛ Need a lesson in how to blow-dry your hair? At Kate's hairdressers, the Richard Ward Salon, £120 will buy you a 75-minute style workshop so that you can achieve salon-beautiful hair at home. After an in-depth consultation about your hair's condition and needs, you are taught how to style your hair like the professionals. Your stylist will blow-dry half your hair and then you style the other half under their expert guidance! A bargain price if you want to re-create Kate's look day in, day out!

Got frizzy hair? Still struggling to master Kate's hair do? You could always get a Brazilian blowout at your hair salon. It improves the condition of your hair and leaves it smooth and frizz-free with a radiant shine.

The Photos

'THEY ARE IN THEIR PRIME AND BRIMMING WITH HAPPINESS. I HAVE NEVER FELT SO MUCH JOY AS WHEN I SEE THEM TOGETHER.'

Mario Testino, photographer

To mark their engagement Kate and William released two official photos. Peruvian born Mario Testino took the portraits at St James's Palace. Mario has created some of the most famous images of Diana, Princess of Wales and has taken some historic images of Prince William, Prince Harry, and Prince Charles. Prince William posed for Mario on his 21st birthday in 2003, Harry posed for him in his 20th birthday a year later, and Prince Charles posed for Mr. Testino to mark his first wedding anniversary to the Duchess of Cornwall.

Lucky Mario can also list Claudia Schiffer, Gisele Bündchen, Elizabeth Hurley, Kate Moss, Emma Watson, Cameron Diaz, Gwyneth Paltrow and Julia Roberts as clients.

The casual photo William and Kate selected to mark their engagement was an affectionate portrait, with Diana's large sapphire and diamond engagement ring prominently on display. They both chose casual clothes to mark the occasion. Both William and Kate wore jeans, with William completing his outfit with a white Turnbull & Asser shirt and brown Cucinelli jumper and Kate finishing her look off in a white Whistles blouse.

The second photograph chosen by the royal pair was a formal shot and their choice of clothing reflected this. Kate wore a white Reiss dress, Links pearl earrings and again the ring was clearly visible. The picture was taken in St James's Palace council chamber. The Palace council chamber is home to several paintings and photographs of some of William's famous ancestors.

A Royal Location

❀ When Zara Philips got engaged, shortly after William and Kate, she and her fiancée Mike Tindall held a spontaneous photo shoot in their garden at their Gloucestershire home instead of having their official photo shot at a royal location.

❀ Zara's father, Captain Mark Phillips, and her mother Princess Anne posed in the grounds of Buckingham Palace for their official photograph. But in a departure from protocol, the couple took their second informal photograph in a meadow away from Buckingham Palace.

❀ After a five-year courtship, Prince Edward asked Sophie Rhys-Jones to become his wife. They marked their special occasion with a photo shoot in the gardens of St James's Palace on 6 January 1999.

❀ Queen Elizabeth's sister Princess Margaret and Anthony Armstrong-Jones were photographed touring Windsor Lodge, marking their official engagement.

❀ Charles and Diana followed royal protocol, releasing an official and unofficial photograph. The official picture, taken at Highgrove, featured Diana in a regal, green gown and Prince Charles in his naval uniform and their unofficial photo, taken at the Palace, was relaxed and laidback with both Diana and Charles in matching sky-blue shirts.

The Press, Diana and Kate

THE PRESS

As Kate and William stepped out for their engagement press conference, they were showered with good wishes and overwhelmed by flashing bulbs. The public and press alike received the news enthusiastically. In fact, the huge amount of press attention highlighted to the world the social, cultural, and historic significance of the occasion. But gravely, it also drew attention to the serious implications of their future as a married couple under the glaring eye of the press and public.

Just how much will Kate's life change when she becomes part of the royal household?

Kate is perhaps better prepared for life as a married royal than some of the other royal wives as she has had time to adjust to life under the spotlight. Spending eight years at William's side, Kate will have learnt to deal with some, but not all, of the intense media interest and constant public curiosity surrounding their relationship. She will also have become familiar with the necessary security procedures and protocol that surrounds William, putting her in good stead for a future under royal protection.

'KATE HAS NOT PUT A FOOT WRONG. SHE APPEARS MODEST AND BEAUTIFUL, AND IS LIKED BY THE PRESS. THERE IS A BREEZY UNPRETENTIOUSNESS ABOUT HOW SHE LOOKS AND WHAT SHE WEARS. THE PERFECT PRINCESS-IN-WAITING.'

Geordie Greig, editor of Tatler

For William, life under the media's watchful eye will continue much the same as it always has. William grew up protected by press advisors and royal protection and because of this; he is comfortable in front of the camera and surrounded by the press. However, for Kate it is a different story. As a young girl dreaming of marrying her prince charming, Kate would not have imagined the darker side of being a princess or considered the intense pressure of the worldwide media. Yet from the moment she accepted William's hand in marriage, she in turn accepted a brand new life for herself. Kate will need to learn the ropes and adjust quickly if she is to cope with her new life. But with an experienced and media-savvy William by her side to guide her, it shouldn't take her too long!

The first difference Kate will have noticed is the round-the-clock security provided by Scotland Yard. As a member of the royal family, a bodyguard will always accompany Kate wherever she goes. This will have a huge effect on her social life. Kate will no longer be able to do things on her own as she has done in the past, so it will be important that she keep her friends closer than ever.

Kate will also have to accept that she is now a public servant and a role model to millions; her every movement will be scrutinised. For 21st-century girls, Kate has a lot of appeal. She is down-to-earth, straightforward, confident, genuine and intelligent. As a royal couple, William and Kate are adorable and have a wide appeal. They are young and more informal than other royals making them much more likeable and personable. If Kate is to accept her new role as a leading lady, she should continue to be herself and let her personality and style sparkle through.

Lucky for Kate she has a great set of gal pals and a fantastic, loyal sister who she can trust and rely on, who will be able to carry her through the hard times. But it will be her love for William that will carry her through life, knowing he will always be by his side.

DIANA

'SHE IS AN INSPIRATIONAL WOMAN TO LOOK UP TO.'

Kate on Diana

If marrying into centuries of tradition isn't a big enough weight on Kate's shoulder, one of the hardest things she will have to deal with is the comparisons to William's mum, Princess Diana.

'THERE'S NO PRESSURE. IT'S ABOUT CARVING HER OWN FUTURE. NO ONE IS TRYING TO FILL MY MOTHER'S SHOES.'

William

The Media

'KATE HAS NOT PUT A FOOT WRONG. SHE APPEARS MODEST AND BEAUTIFUL, AND IS LIKED BY THE PRESS.'

Geordie Greig, editor of Tatler

There has never been a single person in history that has dominated the front pages of the media as much as Princess Diana did. All around the world, whenever her picture graced the cover of a magazine or newspaper that publication would enjoy record-breaking sales. Diana was simply the most famous and most photographed person in the world. No matter what Diana did she could not shake off the fact she was famous. The job she performed for her country was exceptional and unique and so her premature death had a profound impact on the world.

Diana has continued to be close to the public's hearts since her death in 1997. While the whole nation mourned for the loss of the 'People's Princess', there was also a backlash against the royal family and the paparazzi. As far as the public were concerned, on that fateful night in Paris, the paparazzi had acted like wild animals. In fact, for most of her life, the press had hounded Diana, and in the months leading up to her death the paparazzi had become even more menacing. They simply could not get enough of her and were relentless in their pursuit.

'I NEVER KNOW WHERE A LENS IS GOING TO BE.'
HRH The Princess of Wales, Panorama, 20 November 1995

After her death, the public, the royal family, and the press alike all learned a lesson. In hindsight they could see the difficulties Diana endured and the constant strain she was under. People don't want to make the same mistakes with Kate. And they would have a hard job doing so. A law was passed to protect the royal family's privacy after Diana's death and so, as William's wife, Kate will also be protected by law. The benefit of this for Kate is that, although she will always be compared to Diana, she will not have to endure the same level of harassment as Diana endured in her private life.

Kate also has the advantage of being older and wiser as she embarks on her life as a member of the royal family. She is able to look at what Diana did right and wrong under the media's watchful eye, and use her mistakes and successes as lessons. Kate will be able to embrace the media and enter the royal family with her eyes open, unlike Diana who was young and naive.

Relationships

❀ Diana was 12 years younger than Charles when she married him aged 20 in 1981, whereas Kate is a few months older than William and is far more mature than Diana was.

❀ Charles's interests and friends were different from Diana's. Kate and William, however, share mutual university friends and enjoy similar activities including skiing, rowing and polo.

❀ Diana married a man who she did not really know. Kate's love for William has been cemented during their eight years of courting. During those eight years, Kate was able to get to know William as a friend first and then a boyfriend; they even had the opportunity to live together while they were friends at university.

❀ Like Diana, Kate will have only one specific job requirement as princess and that will be to provide William with an heir. Diana was lucky enough to be blessed with two sons, William and Harry. William and Kate have spoken openly about their wish to start a family, with William confirming that they would like to start a family after the wedding: 'Obviously we want a family and will have to start thinking about that.'

'WE ENDED UP BEING FRIENDS FOR A WHILE AND THAT WAS A GOOD FOUNDATION BECAUSE I DO GENUINELY BELIEVE NOW THAT BEING FRIENDS WITH ONE ANOTHER IS A MASSIVE ADVANTAGE. IT JUST WENT FROM THERE AND OVER THE YEARS I KNEW THINGS WERE GETTING BETTER AND BETTER.'

Kate

Lifestyle and Charity Work

Diana was a very personable royal. She was very at ease meeting people from different backgrounds to her own. Part of her appeal was the sympathy, natural compassion, and empathy she showed towards people. Diana took certain charities to her heart and tried to make the public aware of their plight. Over the last few years, Kate has become closely associated with the Starlight Children's Foundation, which aims to brighten the lives of seriously ill youngsters. Party Pieces, the business owned by Kate's parents, Michael and Carole, helps Starlight organise events for children. It is thought that Kate will follow in Diana's footsteps and become an ambassador for various charities and attend events to raise awareness of their work.

Her devotion to helping charities is not the only thing Kate has in common with Diana. Kate loves watching William play polo, as did Diana when she was married to Charles. Kate is also a huge fan of tennis and skiing, both of which Diana used to do in her spare time.

Fashion

'SHE'S GOT A GREAT STYLE TO HER…SHE KNOWS WHAT SHE'S DOING, SHE'S SMART, SHE'S OLDER - IT'S NOT LIKE PRINCESS DIANA AT 19. I THINK SHE'S LOOKED GORGEOUS SO FAR.'

Joan Rivers, *The Cut*

Fortunately for Kate, she is older than Diana was at the time of her engagement and she has made her transition from scruffy student to royal princess almost seamlessly. Diana was much younger and it took some time, and a couple of fashion blunders, for her to find her personal style.

Alexandra Shulman, editor of *Vogue*, said of Kate: 'I think Kate is a contemporary version of Diana. She has the same mainstream style and will go on, like Diana, to get more glamorous.' The fashion world has gone crazy for Kate but even in the fashion stakes Kate can't help but be compared to Diana. Despite Kate being well and truly on the way to becoming a 21st-century style icon and modern-day princess the comparisons with some of Diana's iconic, statement outfits are really quite striking.

Diana frequently stood out from the crowd wearing her favourite shades of royal blues, vibrant pinks, sultry reds, and emerald greens and Kate, too, has been spotted at important royal occasions wearing the most vivacious co_____ N_ one in the room could miss Kate when she stepped out _____ _____ the Boodles Boxing Ball, in aid _____ _o one could have missed Dia_____ Milan, Italy.

The roya_____ it also follows the rule of star_____ _ate has a beautiful symmetric_____ Diana was often photograp_____ _here is a striking similarity _____ Day service outfit and Kate's _____ _een wearing a dark brown an_____ _mper, accessorising with matc_____ _at and a pair of drop earrings _____ paying homage to Diana's o_____ _oat, except in beige and brow_____ _leting the look with matching _____ drop earrings. The similarit__

When Kate attended the Sovereign's Parade at the Royal Military Academy Sandhurst to watch William passing out, her outfit had strikingly obvious similarities with the iconic red ensemble which Diana wore to the Christmas church service at Sandringham in 1993. From the eye-popping red coat to the black accessories and Philip Treacy hat, Kate embodied Diana's look perfectly.

Even off-duty, similarities between Kate and Diana can be found.

As a royal princess and future Queen, Kate will have access to the royal vaults and the wonderful jewels kept inside them. Traditionally, princesses also receive new pieces of jewellery from foreign heads of state. Diana, for instance, received an extraordinary number of diamond and sapphire gifts from the Saudi Arabian royal family and on her wedding day, she received a diamond tiara hung with 19 white pearls from the Queen. Kate may even get a similar gift if she is lucky!

Kate effortlessly integrates her fashion and jewellery much as Diana did. Classic dresses are accessorised with small charms, which suits her chic, conservative look and dazzling drop earrings are paired with bold bright Issa London dresses for glamorous evening events. When Diana became a princess, she often paired royal gems with quirky pieces, so we may even see Kate follow suit in the coming months and years.

The one massive similarity in the two women's fashion choices to date has to be that incredible 18-carat sapphire and diamond engagement ring. Prince Charles originally gave the ring to Diana on their engagement day. Prince William said giving Kate the ring was his way of ensuring his late mother could be part of the occasion. In front of the world's press, he said: 'It is very special to me. It was my way to make sure my mother did not miss out on today and the excitement that we are going to spend the rest of our lives together.'

Family jewels are meant to be passed down through the generations, so in the future, we might see more of Diana's jewels, with a modern twist, being modelled by Kate.

Steal the style

'I'VE ALWAYS FELT THAT ANY GIRL COULD BECOME A PRINCESS. IT'S MY PLEASURE TO OFFER A RING THAT HAS BECOME A ROYAL SENSATION. HAVING A LONG RELATIONSHIP WITH THE BRITISH ROYAL FAMILY, I WISH THE COUPLE A LONG AND HAPPY MARRIAGE.'

Kenneth Jay Lane, jeweller for the QVC replica ring

♛

If you want a ring like Kate's without the huge price tag (it was valued at £28,000 or $65,000 back in 1981) there are plenty of replicas on the market. But the best has to be QVC's 'Princess Simulated Sapphire Ring'. It comes in a range of sizes and it even has a lifetime manufacturer's warranty.

♛

In New York, $1000 replica royal wedding engagement rings have been selling fast for The Natural Sapphire Company, Midtown.

♛

In addition to high-street jewellers and QVC, online auction site eBay is also selling replica royal wedding engagement rings for around £120 or $200.

♛

But you'd better be quick, because these replica rings are flying off the shelves!

As part of the Windsor family, Kate will have to take on an active public role. Of course, she won't be the only royal lady performing public duties. Many of the other royal princesses have an active public life that involves a lot of mingling.

Princess Alexandra is the second child and only daughter of the late Duke and Duchess of Kent. In her role as Princess, Alexandra is Patron or President of several organisations. Princess Alexandra also trained in nursing and many of the charities she is an ambassador for reflect this. Princess Alexandra is Patron of Alzheimer's Society, St. Christopher's Hospice, Queen Alexandra's Royal Naval Nursing Service, Cancer BACUP, MIND, Mental Health Foundation, and Cystic Fibrosis Trust. Not only that, but Princess Alexandra has also acted as Counsellor of State in the Queen's absence abroad. She is a busy lady!

Queen Elizabeth's daughter Anne, the Princess Royal, also has a wide range of public roles and a busy working schedule. According to the official website for the British monarchy, Anne began to undertake public engagements alone when she was just 18 and had left school. Her first state visit was in 1969, when she accompanied the Queen and the Duke of Edinburgh to Austria. The Princess Royal is also President of the Save the Children Fund and this was the first major charity with which she became closely associated. In her work for the organisation, the Princess has visited Save the Children projects in many countries, including Indonesia, China, Cambodia, Vietnam, Ethiopia, Malawi, Botswana and Madagascar.

CHARITY WORK

It looks as though Kate will follow in Anne and Alexandra's shoes and continue to do work for the charities she feels most passionate about. Kate is extremely generous with her time and has the makings of a very popular ambassador for several charities. Even before accepting an official role in the royal family, Kate has worked closely with a few charities in the past, devoting her time and money to raise awareness of their plight, especially Starlight Children's Foundation. Generosity certainly runs in the Middleton family as well as the Windsor family.

In 2009 Kate, elegantly regal in a grey halter neck gown, hosted a table of guests at an auction for the Starlight Children's Foundation. The black tie event cost £100 a head and was held at London's Saatchi Gallery. To help raise money for the worthwhile cause, Carole and Michael Middleton also donated a party for 20 youngsters as one of the evening's prizes. On another occasion, Kate helped to organise the Boodles Boxing Ball – a society fight night attended by William, his younger brother Prince Harry and Harry's then girlfriend Chelsy Davy. The evening attracted around 800 guests and raised more than £100,000.

From the grey halter gown she wore to the Saatchi Gallery to the

stunning pink gown at the Boodles Boxing Ball, whenever Kate has stepped out into the limelight for charity events, she has always been occasion-appropriate – even if this has meant wearing a couple of questionable outfits. Two of her outfits have certainly been sensational to say the least, and not in the demure sense of the word! Kate will never be able to escape the image of herself strutting down the catwalk in a sheer dress, showing off her bandeau bra and knickers on the St Andrews charity catwalk. However, even though the outfit was a fashion disaster, it served its purpose; it raised money for a good cause and it attracted the attention of Prince William! And if that wasn't enough it also gave Kate a likeability factor. She has shown the world that she is a very down-to-earth girl with a great sense of humour and is therefore a perfect match for Prince William.

But if any outfit was going to express Kate's great sense of humour and the fact that she has the confidence to wear something without worrying what people think of her, it was the sequined day-glo hot pants and green sparkly halter top she wore to the 1980s-inspired roller disco charity event for Tom Ward at the Children's Hospital in Oxford.

Kate raised a few eyebrows when she dared to bare in fluoro-yellow micro-shorts, a bright green sequin halter neck and Fame-style pink leg-warmers. Her friends also showed their support with Holly Branson daring to wear a tangerine body suit and fuchsia pink tutu, and Kate's sister Pippa flaunting a black sequined dress, sparkly pink leg warmers and matching baby pink shades. Even though all the girls' outfits were daringly absurd, they still managed to look sensational in their retro gear, especially Kate,

whose outfit showed off her slim and striking figure and enviably toned legs.

However, the days of tight hot pants and see-through dresses are probably over for Kate, as every sartorial choice she makes from now on will have great implications. When Kate and William attended the Teenage Cancer Trust charity fundraising gala, their first event together as an engaged couple, Kate wore a mid-length black-and-white monochrome dress by Temperley and a fitted black velvet jacket. And although the outfit was smart and stylish, in keeping with the event, it is a sign of what to expect from Kate's future outfits.

Of course Kate won't devote all her time to charities; she will still enjoy socialising and joining in with other royal pastimes like going to the races, attending royal weddings and holidaying in Balmoral. She is also likely to be asked to several opening ceremonies and special events around the world, like the one she attended in 2006 at the Bluebird in Chelsea, although she will be much busier now and will have to be far more selective with her choices. Kate looked stunning in a baby pink velvet cropped jacket and flimsy floral summer dress when she attended the Bluebird opening.

Being a princess is about moving in the right circles and being seen in the right places and Kate has had plenty of practise when it comes to most royal activities. She has been invited to and attended several important royal engagements and each time has worn a selection of outfits that have been classic and appropriate for the occasion. She always has her finger on the fashion pulse when it comes to choosing her outfit.

POLO

Polo has long played an important part in the Windsor household with Prince Charles, Prince William and Prince Harry all enjoying a spot of polo playing. Kate has often been seen watching William at many polo events with her close circle of friends including her sister Pippa, while enjoying a glass or two of champagne to toast the day.

ORDER OF THE GARTER

Each year in June, a procession and service takes place at Windsor Castle for the Order of the Garter. The Order is the senior and oldest British Order of Chivalry, founded by Edward III in 1348. The Queen attends the service along with other members of the royal family in the Order, including the Duke of Edinburgh, the Prince of Wales, Prince William, the Duke of York, the Earl of Wessex, the Princess Royal, the Duke of Gloucester, the Duke of Kent and Princess Alexandra.

Kate was seen at the Order of Garter in 2008 sharing a joke with Prince Harry and chatting with the Duchess of Cornwall, Camilla. As William's wife, Kate is likely to be seen at the event in the future. A limited number of tickets are available for members of the public to watch the procession to St. George's Chapel from inside the precincts of Windsor Castle. If you are fortunate enough to get hold of tickets and you need some style inspiration, look for a stylish outfit similar to Kate's spotty tailored jacket and skirt combination. Team this with a fancy hat – think big, bold, and matching. Keep it traditional, like Kate, but add a modern quirky twist – something like the black and white feathers she wore on her simple and chic black hat – and accessorise with a pearl bracelet and delicate necklace.

THE RACES

Even before accepting William's hand in marriage, Kate had befriended a few royal ladies. Kate has often been spotted mingling with Tara Palmer-Tomkinson and Zara Phillips at various engagements. At the Cheltenham Racecourse, Zara and Kate were occasion-appropriate. Zara, the glamorous equestrian, opted for failsafe trench coat and brown knee-high boots, while Kate played it safe and traditional in a tweed ensemble. If you are going to the Cheltenham Racecourse, it is best to keep your look traditional like Zara and Kate but if you are going to Ascot then you can be a bit more playful with your outfit.

Live the Life

If you want to spend a fun day at the races and mingle with royalty like Kate, here are some tips and advice on how to place a bet.

♔

1. Look at your race card and select a race and horse you would like to bet on. If you really want to win serious money, swat up on your horses beforehand by reading professionals' opinions on the horses and studying the winning form for each horse.

2. Now, decide whether you would like to place a bet to win or place a bet each-way. Placing a bet to win means the horse has to come first to win any money. If you are not sure if your horse will win you should place a bet each-way as it means that if the horse finishes in first, second or third place you win some money, although this does depend on how many runners up there are.

3. Go to the bookmaker and hand over your betting card with the name of the horse, the amount of money you want to place and the type of bet you have decided on. You can bet big or small.

4. The bookmaker will hand you back a copy of the betting slip. Check that your slip is correct before leaving. You will then need to keep your slip safe.

5. Sit back with a glass of champagne, soak up the atmosphere, and watch the race.

6. If your horse places, return to the bookmaker, hand in your slip and collect your winnings. Unfortunately, if your horse fails to place you haven't won anything.

> In 1711, Queen Anne was out horse riding near Windsor Castle, when she came across an area of open moorland. She was the first person to see the potential for a racecourse at East Cote, which is now famously called Ascot.

Exercise and Workouts

SPORTS

Even though Kate will now be super busy as a leading royal figure, she will still need to keep fit and active to look the part. From a young age Kate enjoyed taking part in different sports – so much so that she continued to keep active at university, going for morning runs, cycling regularly and taking part in rowing races. It's hardly surprising then that Kate has a slight, athletic frame and is physically in good shape.

Want to be as slender as Kate? It's easy. It has been shown that doing as little as thirty minutes of aerobic exercise three times per week can have amazing health benefits. Try to take up some of Kate's favourite sporting activities to help achieve that perfect athletic figure.

The sporty hockey captain

While at college, Kate was head of the hockey team. Hockey requires an excellent level of fitness and stamina, muscular endurance and agility.

Cycling enthusiast

It has been said that Kate cycles for up to an hour a day, often cycling to and from her favourite gym. According to many fitness experts, cycling is one of the best forms of exercise available and offers several benefits.

It is great as a cardiovascular exercise as it gives your body a quick and vigorous workout. As a result of cycling, there is obvious shaping, toning and firming of the thighs, the buttocks, the calf muscles and the stomach. Fat is also replaced by muscle and some studies have suggested that cycling is one of the few exercises that can help reduce cellulite from the thigh region. If you cycle outdoors, it also stimulates your skin and gives you a fresh rosy glow. No wonder Kate always looks refreshed and radiant!

Ski sensation

Skiing isn't for everyone but for members of the royal family it is practically a requirement! Kate is regularly spotted in glamorous locations around the world having fun on the slopes and showing off her seasoned skills. Skiing is a physically demanding sport but is another great cardiovascular activity that tones your entire body and burns loads of calories.

Charity boat races

Kate did a lot of rowing when training for a charity boat race in 2007. She trained to row across the English Channel, which is around 23 miles and no easy feat. Not only did she manage to raise money for a great cause but she also toned up and shed a few pounds in the process.

Steal the style

If you love to ski and want to get Kate's sporty Sloane Square look then think sweet, sensible and stylish.

Kate's practical red Schoffel ski jacket, and black salopettes are spot on for that sophisticated royal look. Try shopping the Stella McCartney ski range for Adidas if you want to replicates Kate's style. And don't be caught in a blizzard without a pair of Bollé goggles. If you're trying to achieve the Kate look on a budget, check out Tesco's Elevation Snow range for ski jackets and TK Maxx which has out of season, designer ski wear and thermals at affordable prices.

Don't forget to pack attire for all the *après-ski* action. Think jeans and a faux fur gilet teamed with a pair of relaxed boyfriend jeans to channel Kate's look.

KATE'S BIKINI BODY

Kate has been seen in her bikini on a few occasions including the time she was photographed on a yacht in her bikini. But it wasn't the first time she has shown off her enviable figure. It's hard not to forget the time she strutted down the catwalk in her bra and knickers showing off her fantastically fit and athletic, healthy body. It was all the proof we need to know that all those hours of physical training really do pay off.

IT'S NOT ALL ABOUT THE PERFECT BODY

Ten alternative reasons to exercise

1. It gives a sense of well being.
2. It improves circulation and promotes healthy skin and hair.
3. Exercising will improve your concentration.
4. It reduces stress.
5. It releases endorphins giving you the feel good factor.
6. It gives you more confidence. If you look good, you feel good.
7. It's a good way to meet new people with shared interest and could even lead to a future romance.
8. You will increase your chances of a good night's sleep and banish those under eye bags.
9. You will no longer have to deprive yourself of the foods you fancy, meaning that coffee and cake is not off the menu.
10. Exercising regularly means you will have more stamina and energy for long shopping trips with your girlfriends.

ALTERNATIVE WORKOUTS

Not everyone has the time or money to exercise like a princess but there are alternative ways to keep fit like Kate, have fun, and not break the bank.

❀ Rowing is an excellent way to get fit and lose weight but it can be a difficult sport to get involved in. Gyms often offer excellent rowing machine facilities, which will give you all the physical and mental benefits of rowing without actually having to cross the Channel.

❀ If you have never skied before, or you simply can't afford a luxury ski break away, you can always go to a dry ski slope to get fit and healthy. Dry ski slopes mimic the attributes of real snow slopes and enable people to ski as if they were on real snow. The ski centres also offer lessons to people who have never skied before, so if you fancy one day being able to hit the slopes with William and Kate, head to your nearest ski centre and get practising.

❀ If skiing really doesn't push your *piste* buttons, you can always try ice skating classes. Classes are inexpensive and they offer great health benefits, including building up endurance, improving your balance, toning your muscles and exercising your mental control.

❀ Although cycling can be an inexpensive hobby, if you already have access to a gym with cycling machines, you can get all the benefits of cycling without owning a bike. Most gyms also offer spinning classes and sometimes you don't need membership to join in, you can go on a pay-as-you-go basis. Spinning classes can be good fun, with various light and music settings being used to create an energised atmosphere. It can also be less monotonous than cycling on a machine by yourself.

Instructors guide you through workout phases, which incorporate a mixture of warm-ups, sprints, climbs, and cool-downs. Otherwise, purchasing a bike is a great investment. It is a versatile machine that is designed to minimise stress as well as maximise exercise efficiency and is also great at providing an alternative, environmentally friendly mode of transport.

- You don't have to completely copy Kate's exercise regimes to get her healthy, slender body. There are alternatives out there that will shape and sculpt your figure.

- Dancing is a great way for people of all ages to get and stay in shape. Flexibility, although often neglected, is an important part of being healthy. Dancing requires a great amount of flexibility in order to achieve a full range of different positions. Bending and stretching are essential components of dance so you naturally become more flexible with practise. Dancing will also improve your balance and posture. An improved posture will instantly give the impression of a smaller frame and give you the confidence you need to stand out from the crowd.

- You can walk your way to health. The beauty of walking is that it can be slotted into your daily routine. Walking can also increase your muscle tone, increase metabolism, relieve stress, raise energy levels and improve sleep.

- Running is another cheap form of exercise and a great cardiovascular workout. Gordon Ramsay, Nigella Lawson, and Katie Price are among the list of celebrities who love it.

- Pilates focuses on rebalancing the body and improving posture through deliberate, controlled movements and exercises.

- Yoga can improve your physical health and wellbeing. Through a series of postures and breathing exercises, yoga helps to develop strength, balance, coordination, and flexibility.

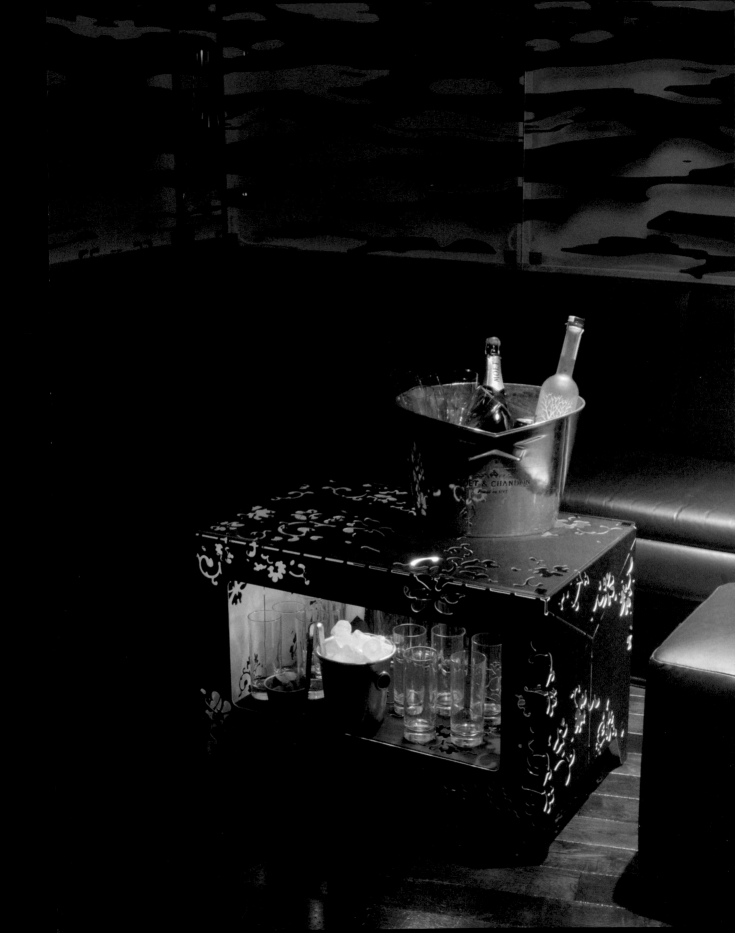

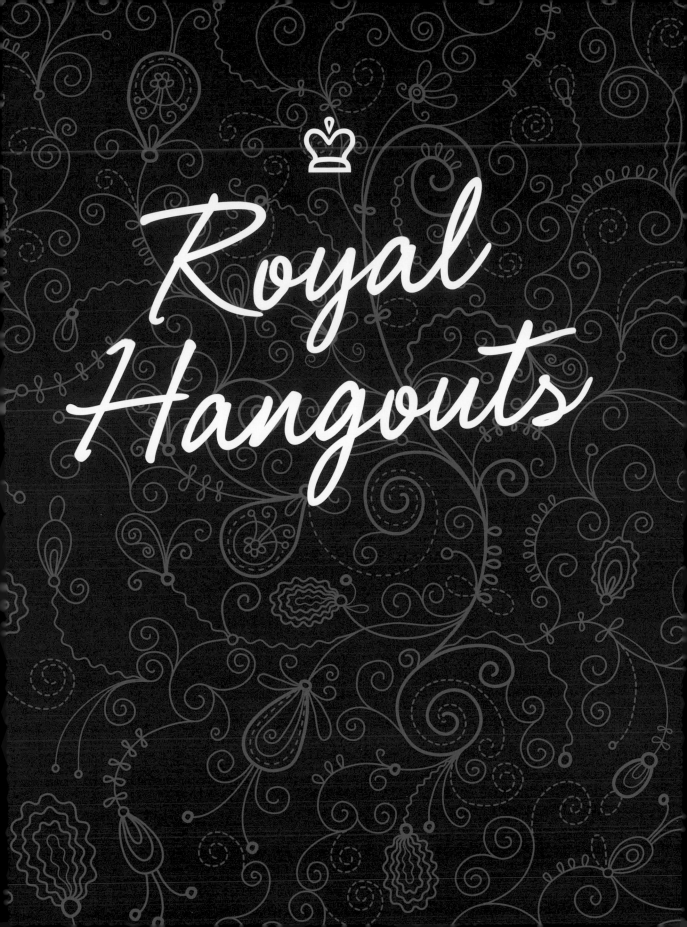

Royal Hangouts

Discover Kate's secret ski resorts, take a walk in her shoes along London's King's Road, join her for a royal night on the tiles and relax in the royal box at some of the most prestigious sporting events in the United Kingdom.

ROYAL RESORTS

Over the years, skiing has played a major role in the lives of the British royal family. It has proved to be the ideal location for winter getaways, family holidays and has sealed the stamp of approval for future royal relationships. It seems as though nowhere is more romantic than a ski resort for the Windsor household.

In 1981, an image of Lady Diana skiing with Prince Charles and his royal party was symbolic of her arrival on the public stage and sparked rumours of an imminent engagement. A few years later, an invitation was extended to Sarah Ferguson to join Charles and Diana at Charles' favourite ski resort, Klosters. Her inclusion was the stamp of approval needed to seal her status as a future member of the royal family and soon after her trip, Prince Andrew asked for Sarah's hand in marriage.

So in 2004, it came as no surprise when William followed in the Windsor family tradition. Kate was invited to join William at Klosters ski resort: a favourite with the royal family. It's a good job Kate was already an accomplished skier and an extremely sporty person! To the world, William's actions were a symbolic declaration of his love for Kate and proof of her acceptance within the royal family.

As you can image the royals, predictably, favour the ritziest resorts and slickest slopes around Europe. They are places for the privileged, full of glamorous hotels, sophisticated men and well turned out women wearing only the latest designer ski clobber.

Want to find yourself a royal who hasn't been spoken for yet? Or mimic

the life of a princess? You had better make sure your skiing skills are on par with Kate's superb skills and treat yourself to a luxurious skiing break at some of these swanky ski resorts.

Klosters

Location: Switzerland

Who goes there? Lord Bamford, the King and Queen of Sweden, Tara Palmer-Tomkinson, Prince Andrew, Prince Harry, Prince William and Kate Middleton.

Ski-trips to Klosters have been a fixture in the royal diary since the late 1970s when the Prince of Wales first visited the Swiss resort. Conventional and lavish, Klosters leads the way as the royal hot spot.

Lech am Arlberg

Location: Austria

Who goes there? Queen Beatrix and the Dutch royal family.

High up in the Arlberg valley lies one of Austria's most alluring resorts, the sedate Lech. The traditional village lies on the banks of a river, with a large collection of four and five-star hotels. It was once a favourite with Princess Diana and has been described as the place to go, offering simple, flattering pistes.

Zermatt

Location: Switzerland

Who goes there? William and Kate, Robbie Williams, Madonna, Sarah Ferguson with Princess Beatrice and Princess Eugenie.

Zermatt is another exceptional Swiss ski resort. It is scenically considered the most beautiful ski resort in the world, especially as it lies at the foot of the Matterhorn. Its glorious scenery makes it an exceptionally romantic location (although this is supposedly where William and Kate ended their relationship in 2007!) Head to the Heimberg Bar and Brown Cow Pub to keep warm after a day on the slopes, and for a chance to rub shoulders with William and Kate.

Verbier

Location: Switzerland

Who goes there? Sir Richard Branson, Ronan Keating, Leonardo DiCaprio, Al Pacino, William, Kate and Sarah Ferguson.

Verbier is recognised as one of the premiere off-piste locations worldwide. At Verbier, it is easy to take advantage of the sheer slopes, varied conditions and the lively nightlife. Sarah Ferguson has strong links to the Verbier ski resort. Before marrying Prince Andrew she lived at Verbier with Paddy McNally, her millionaire lover, and she has been a regular visitor ever since. Her daughter Princess Eugenie celebrated her 18th birthday in the resort, along with her sister Princess Beatrice. Harry, William and Kate have also skied together on the Verbier slopes.

Méribel

Location: France

Who goes there? Prince Felipe of Spain, Roman Abramovich, the Beckhams and Prince Edward.

Prince Edward, as patron of the British Ski and Snowboard Federation, visits ski resort Méribel every March, together with the Countess of Wessex, Sophie. From Méribel it is easy and convenient to explore the 200 lifts, 130 km of Cross Country tracks and 600km of piste that creates the Trois Vallées.

PARTY LIKE A PRINCESS: NIGHTCLUBS

Married life in North Wales means that Kate won't be able to enjoy London life as much as she used to, particularly the London club scene. Although it shouldn't be too difficult for Kate to leave the scene behind her because on the advice of the Queen, William and Kate have withdrawn more and more from London's lavish lifestyle in favour of a more relaxed life in Wales. Besides, despite a penchant for London nightlife, Kate, like a true royal pro, has always managed to retain a squeaky-clean image when it comes to her partying.

In the past, Kate was regularly spotted visiting some of London's priciest venues, where she was always welcomed like royalty. If you fancy partying like a princess, spotting A-List celebrities and rubbing shoulders with royalty try hitting up some of these distinguished venues.

Boujis

Location: South Kensington, London

Boujis, according to their website, is the award-winning premium nightlife brand. Boujis has played host to a consistent international mix of the who's-who of film, music, fashion, sport and royalty – plus local London celebrities and VIPs.

Prince William and Harry have been regulars at the club for some time now and Kate has been spotted leaving the trendy London club on several occasions especially during her split from Wills in 2007.

Whisky Mist

Location: Mayfair, London

Whisky Mist is another private members only club. In the past, Kate Middleton has been spotted doing a little club-hopping with gal pal Holly Branson and friends at the swanky nightclub. Whisky Mist is also popular amongst footballers including, Cesc Fabregas and Joe Cole.

Mahiki

Location: Dover Street, London

Mahiki is the ultimate destination for the cocktail lover and for some time was a favourite haunt of Kate's. And it is not difficult to see why it was a firm favourite for Kate during her single months. Mahiki creates the illusion of having arrived at a colourful, distant port of pleasure and is decorated with hand-made 'princess' chairs, hand-carved tiki figures, Hawaiian cushions, and green rush affect banquettes. All fit for a princess.

BOUJIS CLASSIC CLUB COCKTAILS

Port Royal Caipirinha
Wray and Nephew overproof rum, fresh lime and vanilla sugar

Champagne Bellini
with peach, raspberry, passion fruit or pear

Steal the Style

Kate's party girl look is simple to emulate and will be easy to find online or on the high street.

When heading for a girly night with your friends think easy to wear dresses with a classic sex appeal. Alternatively try wearing tight skinny jeans and bold bright tops or sophisticated blouses. Keep your jewellery simple, your footwear comfortable but stylish, like black suede boots, and your hair big and bouncy.

For the ultimate Kate party piece, be inspired by geometric prints. Kate has on many occasions worn flirty dresses in geometric prints, giving a nod to 1960s mod fashion.

Tips for wearing geometric prints:

- ♛ Stick to simple accessories. Bold patterns need subtle pieces to complement them.
- ♛ Don't overdo your print mixing. Flowers and animal prints are great patterns, but not in the same outfit.
- ♛ Stick to a neutral palette and opt for a colour scheme that's calm and versatile.

Raffles

Location: Chelsea, London

Everyone loves to get there swagger on and this includes Kate and William, both of whom have been spotted partying in London club Raffles until gone three in the morning.

Raffles claims it will continue to run as a discreet members' club with membership available through interview or recommendation. So if you want to party alongside the royals you better get an invitation to join the party!

Kitts Club

Location: Chelsea, London

In 2008, Kate celebrated her 26th birthday bash at the Sloane Square club, Kitts. She began with a shindig at her apartment in Chelsea followed by a meal at Tom Aikens' Michelin-starred restaurant in South West London. After the meal, Kate headed for Kitts Club in Sloane Square with her sister and friends. What better way to celebrate your birthday?

Despite exiting some of the clubs in the wee hours of the morning, Kate nearly always managed to leave looking her best. It may have been the magic of her youth or the blessings of good bone structure but when leaving the posh clubs early in the morning Kate projected *joie de vivre*, which only some of us can dream of having.

♔♕♔ *Tip* ♔♕♔

TIPS FOR LOOKING YOUR BEST AFTER A NIGHT ON THE TILES

Your skin is often the first thing to suffer. Use a moisture replenishing cream to pep your skin back to life and disguise the fact you've just been propping up the bar.

Don't forget your eyes. Conceal any under-eye dark circles with concealer as this will even out your complexion and instantly brighten your face. Concealer is the single most important thing you can use to lose a tired look so make sure you carry a spare in your bag. Then the following morning, when you have a chance, use a cooling mask to keep the bags at bay.

Blusher is also a great tool to keep in your bag, as it will give your face an instant lift.

Keep your make-up light and natural; wipe away any eyeliner that has managed to crawl down your face, or you run the risk of drawing attention to those dark circles you have just been trying to hide.

By 3am hair often loses its va va voom, so carry a small comb and travel-sized leave-in-conditioner in your handbag and give your hair a quick spritz before you leave the club.

If you've survived the day after a big night out indulge in some serious pampering to rejuvenate yourself.

SHOP LIKE A PRINCESS

From the moment Kate took centre stage at the public announcement of her engagement, the fashion world has been in a frenzy.

All budding princesses looking to copy Kate's much-desired look should head to London and hit the high streets or shop online, both of which are awash with cut-price replicas. But if you can afford the real thing here are some of Kate's favourite shopping haunts.

King's Road and Sloane Square, Chelsea, London

King's Road runs for approximately two miles through Chelsea and incorporates the exclusive Sloane Square. It is Chelsea's high street and one of the most fashionable, popular shopping streets in London. King's Road is a shopping haven, crammed full of beautiful boutiques and high street stores and a place to see the capital's elite and the place to be seen if you are part of the capital's elite.

Kate's style offers perfect examples of luxurious, good taste that is hugely accessible. So it is no surprise that Kate has been seen, many times, walking along London's famous King's Road popping into high street stores.

Links of London

King's Road is home to Links of London's most prestigious and luxurious flagship store. It is tucked away inside the glamorous Sloane Square where it displays the latest Links of London collections for men, women, and children. If you want to get your hands on a pair of earring like the one's Kate wore for her official engagement photographs then head to Links, where a pair of similar earrings will set you back £275.

Reiss

The high-end, high street favourite stands for iconic, sexy, luxurious wear and is popular amongst the elite and masses alike. It is a global brand and can be located all around the world but if you want to catch a glimpse of Kate and walk in her shoes, head to London's King's Road branch. Here you can pick up some wardrobe favourites, including the belted Nanette gown with three-quarter length sleeves and a frill along the zip, which Kate wore for her official engagement photograph. The dress was remade at the end of January and put back into Reiss stores, where 600 dresses were used to replenish the sold-out stock.

Whistles

The Whistles blouse Kate wore for her engagement outfit isn't the only one Kate has been spotted wearing. In fact, Whistles is surely one of Kate's favourite brands, having stepped out in their clothes many a time. The brand has now earned a reputation for creating perfect trouser, must-have dresses as well as the most luxurious knitwear. Whistles is a necessary stop if you are heading to King's Road hoping to emulate Kate's look.

Harrods, Knightsbridge

Home to hundreds of designer brands, Harrods is the ultimate in fashion luxury. It houses concession stands from the likes of Ralph Lauren to Fendi and Prada. But most importantly, it stocks the brand made most famous by Kate, Issa. Issa dresses are highly versatile and are glamorous enough for an evening affair or casual enough for a day spent walking the streets of London on a summer's day. Kate is exceptionally fond of Brazilian designer Daniella Helayel and has frequently worn her Issa dresses. On several occasions, she has worn her creations to important royal functions and charity events. Issa dresses don't come cheap but a visit to Harrods is well worth it to catch a glimpse of royalty from around the world and cast your eye over the latest designs brought to you straight from the catwalk.

Steal the Style

We all know Kate wears Issa dresses like they are going out of fashion. Their trusty figure-hugging designs, nipped in at the waist, and bold block colours flatter Kate perfectly. But sometimes it is easy to get stuck in a style rut. Fortunately, for Kate every Issa dress she has worn to date has looked effortlessly chic and stunningly different on her slender figure. From the gunmetal grey dress to the navel-cut neckline coral dress, Kate has triumphed in the fashion stakes.

Issa London can be bought all over the world. It is available in London at Harrods, Matches, and Harvey Nichols. North American stockists include Neiman Marcus and Nordstrom. A full list of Issa stockists can be found on their website. The designs are timeless and can withstand changes in seasons, so purchasing one of her designs could be a lifetime investment.

If you can't afford the Issa price tag, look out for dresses on your local high street with a distinct Issa feel. Think silk or satin material, to-the-floor hemlines, detailed waists and bold bright block colours.

Notting Hill

Kate doesn't just limit herself to the King's Road. Occasionally she has been seen browsing the shops in and around Notting Hill, counting clothes shop Temperley as a favourite. Temperley has become synonymous with timeless glamour, exquisite designs and must have collections, which are admired by women around the world. Kate chose a classic Temperley design to attend the Teenage Cancer Trust Christmas Spectacular, her first official royal engagement as William's fiancée. The dress embodied all the trademark designs of Temperley including luxurious silks, lace and embroidery. Kate teamed the black and cream dress with classic black pumps, a cropped jacket, and a compact clutch. The knee-length Alice Temperley dress with its nipped in waist was a perfect match for Kate's sophisticated style. Although no longer available, Alice Temperley still has similar dresses in stock, so start adding them to your shopping wish list!

Of course, Temperley isn't the only place in Notting Hill to find Kate-inspired pieces. Kate is an expert in mixing and matching designer labels with thrifty finds. She truly is a 'recessionista'! Head to Portobello Market on a Friday to raid the vintage stands, or on a Saturday to find some real fashion steals! Or trawl the quaint independent shops any day of the week to find affordable dresses, one-of-a-kind pieces of jewellery and sophisticated shoes from independent designers. And if you have time, take a stroll along Westbourne Grove, where you can find plenty of high-end and high-street shops where you can pick out a few signature Kate pieces to complement your market stall buys!

SHOPPING ESSENTIALS

1. Comfortable, flat shoes like Ugg boots or ballet pumps
2. Clothes that can be easily removed so you can try on potential purchases
3. A small bag, preferably designer like her white Prada bag to keep the basics in – mobile, purse and credit cards
4. Your mum, sister or a friend who can give you shopping advice
5. Lastly, if you can afford it – someone to carry your bags!

If all that shopping becomes too much, hit up Starbucks for a caffeine fix. Kate has been spotted sipping on a Starbucks coffee in the past, so if it's good enough for a princess it's good enough for us!

HOLIDAY LIKE A PRINCESS

Sometimes living in the royal goldfish bowl gets stressful, so Kate will be hoping to escape now and again to some of her favourite holiday locations far away from prying eyes and royal duties. In the past, Kate has holidayed at some fantastic locations around the world from Scotland to Kenya.

Royal locations

Mustique, Caribbean

Mustique is an ideal location for royalty because it is an entirely private island containing seven valleys, each with white, sandy, deserted beaches surrounded by a series of coral reefs. The island is far enough south that it is never out of season and so enjoys temperatures of around 75F all year round. It even manages to avoid those dreaded hurricanes!

Mustique was a well-known holiday destination of Princess Margaret and it has attracted a list stars including Johnny Depp and David Bowie. In 2006 and 2009, Kate took a holiday on the Caribbean island.

Kenya, Africa

> 'I'D BEEN PLANNING IT FOR A WHILE BUT AS ANY GUY OUT THERE WILL KNOW IT TAKES A CERTAIN AMOUNT OF MOTIVATION TO GET YOURSELF GOING. I WAS PLANNING IT AND THEN IT JUST FELT REALLY RIGHT OUT IN AFRICA. IT WAS BEAUTIFUL AT THE TIME.'
>
> *William*

Prince William has visited Kenya several times over the years, so it came as no surprise when he took Kate to Kenya on holiday. It was during their romantic break away in the African national park that Prince William proposed to Kate in a secluded log cabin. Their hideaway was part of the Rutundu Log Cabins complex located in the shadow of Mount Kenya. The cosy cabins are in an ideal location for an adventurous but luxe getaway, where activities include fishing on Lake Rutundu and Lake Alice and horse riding on well-schooled polo ponies – so you'll need to be an experienced rider like William!

Ibiza

In 2006, Kate enjoyed a luxurious yacht holiday on the Mediterranean Sea looking out at the island of Ibiza! In a white bikini, Kate enjoyed taking in all the delights of the island from the yacht, staying clear of the well-known summer club parties, which attract large numbers of tourists, she preferred to hang out with her friends who were also on board the yacht.

Balmoral Castle, Scotland

Balmoral Castle and its surrounding estate is a popular destination for the royal family. The private property and holiday home of the royal's is located between the settlements of Braemar and Ballater on a stretch of the River Dee. Although it is used by the royal family in the summer months, it is open to visitors but only during April to July and October to early December. Kate has been whisked away to Balmoral on several occasions and her parents were spotted holidaying at the Castle after the announcement of Kate's engagement to William.

Steal the style

Give your wardrobe a breath of fresh and funky country air, just like Kate's. Taking her inspiration from the countryside, Kate effortlessly adopts a quintessentially British style, which you can easily channel too.

Chunky knits and beautifully cut denim jeans never go out of fashion, so team yours up with tweed, plaid or *faux* fur to create the perfect countryside Kate look. The high street will be awash with Kate inspired pieces and designer Joules will be leading the way.

If you want to create a true royal look, invest in a Barbour jacket, a royal favourite. Anya Hindmarch fur-trimmed Barbour design is the ideal compromise between country bumpkin and city chic. Her design even includes labelled pouches for your lipstick and phone - the perfect touch for a girl on the go!

HOME IS WHERE THE HEART IS

Bucklebury, Berkshire

Kate's childhood home is one location she will never grow tired of and home to Kate will always be her parents' house. Kate will still have a bedroom for when she decides to visit her family and it will be here she

will be able to relax and be scruffy away from the public. If anybody understands the importance of loyalty, unconditional love, and secrecy, it's Kate. She loves her family home so much she even celebrated her 27th birthday there. And, of course the day was made complete when Prince William joined the celebrations along with Kate's sister Pippa, brother James, and her parents Michael and Carole.

Blaenau Ffestiniog, North Wales

Loved-up Kate and William have set up home in Blaenau Ffestiniog in North Wales, to be close to William's RAF base. Although the exact location of their love-nest has not been revealed, it is likely that it will be

well off the beaten track and is likely to have stunning views of Snowdonia. Although Anglesey is not a large place to live, there are several pubs and restaurants in the area were William and Kate will be able to dine, including the award-winning White Eagle Pub and The Bull Hotel.

SPORTING EVENTS

Kate is very sporty and can often be found skiing down the slopes, rowing on rivers and cycling through the countryside. But Kate is not just keen on playing sport she is also a huge fan of watching sport from tennis at Wimbledon to cheering on her man at a polo match. At every sporting event, Kate never fails in the fashion stakes from flimsy summer frocks to gentry-inspired tailored shirts and skirts she always embodies the perfect royal look.

Polo

Kate Middleton's loyalty to William knows no bounds. Kate told novelist Kathy Lette that she was allergic to horses but she is still regularly spotted cheering for William and his brother Harry on the sidelines. Whenever Kate is seen watching Wills play Polo she always looks chic and elegant – the perfect match for a future King. Whilst attending Polo matches in the summer, Kate tends to favour

wearing summer frocks and designer sunglasses. During the Polo match at Beaufort Polo Club in Gloucestershire, Kate wore a loose light blue-grey dress and a black belt to emphasis her small waist, which she teamed with matching black sunglasses and a bottle of Piper champagne! But Kate has also mastered the art of looking regal and stylish in jeans and a shirt, her outfit at the 'Tusk' Charity Polo Match at Beaufort Polo Club in 2008 is a perfect example. With her tussled hair flowing casually over her left shoulder, Kate's white Ralph Lauren inspired jumper and tight blue jeans give her an imperial, aristocratic appearance. A look more than appropriate for a princess. And she certainly knows that wedges or flat shoes are better than a pair of sky scrapper heels when traipsing across grass!

Tennis

In 2010 Her Majesty the Queen made her first visit to Wimbledon since 1977, her Silver Jubilee year. And Kate has often been spotted enjoying the Wimbledon Tennis Championships from the stands. In 2008 Kate radiated beauty and elegance in a stark white dress, with a trademark

cinched-in waist and small black cardigan. Kate has also been known to enjoy playing a spot of tennis in her spare time so I think we can expect to see her at more tennis events than the Queen.

Horse racing

Even though Kate is said to be allergic to horses, it doesn't stop her going to the races. The Queen who owns a number of flat and jump horses, is a big fan of horseracing, as are many other members of the royal family and aristocracy, so it seems only fitting that Kate too enjoys horseracing. It also means that Kate will have a lot to talk about with the Queen when she visits Buckingham Palace. Polo isn't the only event where Kate makes a special effort to dress the part. At the Cheltenham Horse Racing event, Kate cheered on Denman as he won the Gold Cup wearing a royal blue hat and matching trench coat, blending in superbly with her contemporaries. And at the Cheltenham Festival Horse Race in 2009, Kate and William wore complimentary outfits, both opting for flattering baby blue shirts and tweed jackets. But Kate added a special, modern twist to her outfit with a pair of her favourite Chanel designer sunglasses.

The Wedding

As soon as the announcement was made public, it was being dubbed as the wedding of century. When Kate walks down the aisle to marry her Prince Charming on Friday 29 April, William, it will be the biggest royal event since Prince Charles and Diana wed in 1981. From the design of Kate's dress to the location of the wedding the rumour mill hasn't stopped turning.

When it comes to a royal wedding Kate and William will have a lot to live up to. Many stunning and lavish royal weddings have taken place over the centuries and not just in the United Kingdom. From the choice of venue to the after party celebrations, Kate and William's wedding will undoubtedly draw comparisons to other royal weddings. But as with most weddings it will be the blushing bride who attracts the most attention.

'A HAPPY AND MOMENTOUS OCCASION.'

David Cameron

Kate is in line to become the first commoner to be queen since Anne Hyde wed the Duke of York, later James II, in 1660. Royal consorts have traditionally come from the ranks of Britain's aristocracy. And when she waltzes down the aisle, to live out a fairytale dream come true, all eyes will be on her. The public, the media and fashion editors around the world will be scrutinising her every move from the shape of her dress and the style of her hair to the colour of

On the Party Pieces website, the wonderful family business owned by Kate's parents Carole and Michael, her brother James was asked, 'Have you had any cake disasters?' to which he replied, 'My sister trying to make the cake and forgetting to add the self-raising flour! She ended up using the flat sponge to make a trifle cake instead. Boys don't like trifle when they should have had a pirate cake!' Let's hope Kate and Pippa don't try to help with the wedding cake!

her lipstick. She will be compared to the many other royal brides who have waltzed down the aisle to marry their Prince, not just Princess Diana. But if Kate's closet is anything to go by women around the world won't be disappointed by the bride's choices.

THE LOCATION

The location of the wedding was one of the first important things to be finalised in Kate and William's wedding plans. There appeared to be three main contenders in the running: St. Paul's Cathedral, Windsor Castle and Westminster Abbey.

St Paul's Cathedral

The historic St. Paul's Cathedral, built by Sir Christopher Wren between 1675 and 1710, was a main contender in the running because it had been the focus of many other royal celebrations and historic services in the past including the Queen's Golden Jubilee and her 80th birthday.

The wedding of Lady Diana Frances Spencer and Charles, Prince of Wales, also took place at St Paul's Cathedral on July 29, 1981. At the time, the couple chose the Cathedral as their wedding venue because of its size and ability to accommodate a large number of guests. Diana was 20 years old and Charles 32 years old at the time of their wedding and the couple had invited over 3500 guests to celebrate with them.

> On 29 April 1964 Princess Irene married Spanish Prince Carel Hugo de Bourbon Parma.

Windsor Castle

Windsor Castle, built more that 1000 years ago, was also considered a contender in the running because of its picturesque location. Perched at the top of a hill overlooking the town, the River Thames and Windsor Great Park, it is a place of unimaginable beauty. But it was also considered the least favourite location because it is situated outside of the capital city and it only has space for a small gathering. It would be nowhere near large enough for the huge gathering that William and Kate's wedding will attract. In 1999, St George's Chapel at Windsor Castle was the intimate location of Prince Edward and Sophie Rhys Jones' wedding. Only 560 guests attended their ceremony. The Castle had also been the favoured location of Prince Charles and Camilla, the Duchess of Cornwall for their wedding. In 2005, the couple married at the Guildhall before throwing a party at the Castle.

But the winner was to be Westminster Abbey.

Westminster Abbey

Westminster Abbey is steeped in more than a thousand years of history and has housed many royal ceremonies and historic services. Significantly, The Queen and the Queen Mother both married there. The Queen married Prince Philip of Greece in 1947 and the Queen Mother, then Lady Elizabeth Bowes-Lyon had married the then Duke of York in 1923.

Although Westminster Abbey had been the punters favourite, there had been reason to doubt its suitability. Princess Diana's funeral had been held at the Abbey and it holds painful memories for William and Harry. William will now hope that the Abbey carries both sad and happy memories when he ties the knot with Kate in April. Expect to see around 2000 guests – the Cathedral's capacity!

Kate will be driven by car to Westminster Abbey along the traditional processional route of the Mall, Horse Guards Parade, Whitehall and Parliament Square.

The service, at 11am on 29 April, will be conducted by the Dean of the Abbey, the Very Rev John Hall. The Archbishop of Canterbury, Rowan Williams, will marry the couple and the Right Rev Richard Chartres, the bishop of London and a longstanding friend of the royal family, will give the address.

After the ceremony, Kate and William will return to the Palace along the same route by horse drawn carriage. Once at the Palace it is likely the pair will wave and kiss from the Royal Balcony and give the public one last look at their wedding finery before attending a reception hosted by the Queen

On 29 April 1986 the Duchess of Windsor, Wallis Simpson, was laid to rest alongside her husband, the abdicated King Edward VIII, at Frogmore in Windsor.

inside the palace. In the evening, Prince Charles will host a private dinner followed by dancing for close friends and family.

Carriages fit for a princess

With Kate and William set to depart Westminster Abbey in a horse-drawn coach it is likely the horse and carriage will be chosen from the Royal Mews. Buckingham Palace's official stable yard and carriage house, the Royal Mews, was established in 1761 and has over 100 historic coaches and 34 horses.

The traditional glass coach is the favourite carriage of choice. It was built in 1881and has carried the last three royal brides, Queen Elizabeth, Princess Margaret and Princess Diana to or from their wedding. But Kate will have a choice of more than just the one carriage. She may decide to return to the Palace in the Royal Britannia, which was a gift to the Queen from the Prime Minister of Australia. It is a modern built carriage for a modern day princes with heating and electric windows but it also has historic features including wood taken from historic British ships and cathedrals.

For her arrival at the Abbey, Kate is likely to travel in the open top State Landau, which has been used frequently to transport the monarchy to and from royal ceremonies.

But by whatever means Kate decides to travel she will certainly travel in style and be a picture perfect bride.

ICONIC WEDDINGS

Queen Elizabeth II and Prince Philip, Duke of Edinburgh

When: 20 November 1947.

Where: Westminster Abbey, London.

Officiated by: The Archbishop of Canterbury and the Archbishop of York.

The Dress: The dress was made of ivory duchess satin and decorated with around 10,000 white seed pearls, silver thread, and tulle embroidery. It had a 13-foot patterned full court train starting at the shoulders and a silk tulle veil to match. Her jewellery included a tiara borrowed to her from her mother.

The Bouquet: white orchids and a sprig of myrtle designed by Longmans florist.

The Ring: A band of Welsh gold.

Bridesmaids and Page Boys: Eight bridesmaids and two pageboys.

Guests: over 2000.

The Groom: Royal Navy Uniform.

The Reception: After the ceremony, the Queen and Prince Philip made an appearance on the balcony of Buckingham Palace. Elizabeth's father King George VI and her younger sister Princess Margaret, as well as her grandmother Queen Mary, and her mother, the Queen consort, joined them on the balcony in what has now become an iconic picture. A celebratory lunch was then held at the Palace.

The wedding cake: The cake had four tiers, was nine feet high, and weighed 500 pounds. The cake was cut using Philip's sword.

The Honeymoon: Hampshire, and the Balmoral estate.

Charles, Prince of Wales and Lady Diana Frances Spencer

When: 29 July 1981.

Where: St. Paul's Cathedral, London.

Officiated by: The Archbishop of Canterbury officiated the wedding. 25 other clerics were also present. The service was a traditional Church of England wedding service.

The Dress: Diana's wedding dress was designed by Elizabeth and David Emanuel and was a puffball meringue in design, with matching puffed sleeves and a frilly neckline. The dress was made of silk taffeta and included lace, hand embroidery, sequins, and 10,000 pearls for decoration. The train of the dress was 25 feet long. Diana wore the Spencer family diamond tiara to hold her veil in place.

The Bouquet: Her bouquet was made up of gardenias, lilies of the valley, white freesias, golden roses, white orchids, stephanotis and sprigs of myrtle. It was also designed by Longmans Florists, which has now closed, so expect to see something a bit different for Kate's bouquet.

The Ring: A Welsh gold band.

The Groom: Charles wore his full dress naval commander uniform.

Bridesmaids and Pageboys: Five bridesmaids and two pageboys.

Guests: 3,500 at the ceremony. Another 750 million people watching the ceremony and 250 million people listening on the radio. Two million spectators lined the route of Diana's procession from Clarence House, with 4,000 police and 2,200 military officers used to manage the crowds.

The Reception: Like Queen Elizabeth, Prince Charles and Diana stood on the balcony of Buckingham Palace to greet the well-wishers who had turned up to see them. They then proceeded to enjoy their reception at the Palace with 120 other diners.

The Wedding Cake: The official wedding cake was made up of five tiers but there were also approximately twenty-two other large wedding cakes to share with their guests.

The Honeymoon: Hampshire, a Mediterranean cruise and Balmoral.

Princess Margaret and Anthony Armstrong-Jones

When: 6th May 1960.

Where: Westminster Abbey, London.

Princess Margaret's wedding to Anthony Armstrong-Jones was the first ever royal wedding to be shown on television.

Prince Rainier III and Grace Kelly

When: 19 April 1956.

Where: St. Nicholas Cathedral, Monaco.

Hollywood actress and beauty icon Grace Kelly had met her royal husband-to-be only twice before walking down the aisle with him. Her wedding was the perfect combination of Hollywood glamour and royal tradition.

Prince Edward and Sophie Rhys-Jones

When: 19 June 1999.

Where: St. George's Chapel, Windsor Castle.

There were only 560 guests present at Edward and Sophie's wedding ceremony. Prince Edward designed two things for Sophie to wear on her wedding day – a black-and-white pearl necklace and a dress coat.

THE DRESS

To many, the style and colour of the wedding dress is probably the single most important decision the bride will have to make. From the moment Kate and William announced their engagement, women around the world began to channel their inner Bridezilla through Kate and anxiously they now anticipate the wedding dress of the century.

It's not just the whole female population in a frenzy, practically every designer in the world is willing to dress the bride for her big day. And having the opportunity or not to design the iconic dress, it has not stopped them speculating to *Vogue* magazine about the style, colour and material of the dress. Here's what some of the designers had to say:

Alice Temperley: 'If we were lucky enough to be asked for this amazing task, I would make her into a true English rose: classic, regal and ethereal. Could be the most amazing dress ever designed – God I would love to do it.'

Bruce Oldfield: 'She has such a gorgeous figure that she'd look good in a sack and it would obviously be a huge honour to be entrusted with such an important commission. She has an elegant refined style which is modern and fresh and I would play to all of these points – a simple silhouette, sufficient detailing to give it the sense of occasion but not so much as to drown her slight frame.'

Holly Fulton: 'I would respect the need for tradition and being demure while combining my signature style to give her a dress taking its concept from the principles of Victorian love tokens. These precious stones are used to spell out a love message or someone's name using the first letters of the names of the stones involved, in this instance: W, Water sapphire; I, Indicolite; L, Labradorite; L, Lapis lazuli; I, Iolite; A, Amethyst; M, Moonstone. I would use these stones to create an embellished neckline round a simple, very full silk dress and would also trim round the decorative stone section with freshwater pearls and bead the hem with a single row of these to give it a nice hang. It would be a simple yet intricately embellished piece – I think she will be glowing enough that day not to need anything too ostentatious or contrived.'

Osman Yousefzada: 'A structured one shoulder dress – clean lines and purity with the focus on the texture and craftsmanship of the fabric. And a very simple but graphic architectural veil...looking super chic but effortless.'

The name of the dress designer is, however, being kept under lock and key at St James's Palace until the wedding day. But that designer is likely to be British. Like many other royal brides that have gone before her, it is almost customary for Kate to select home-grown talent to design her dress. Queen Elizabeth, Princess Margaret, and Diana all wore British designs on their big day.

Deborah Joseph, editor of *Bride* magazine, told *Vogue*: 'I think she will wear a British designer but I can't decide whether she'll give a nod to tradition and go for someone classic such as Bruce Oldfield who designs many bespoke gowns for royalty. On the other hand, she may be totally independent and forge her own way, setting herself up as a new fashion icon by choosing a dress designed by someone younger and hipper like Jenny Packham or Alice Temperley. She's a young, modern woman so I think she will like to do her own thing but incorporate a traditional touch; for instance some brides take a piece of jewellery that belonged to someone special and have that sewn into the dress. I imagine she might like to do that.'

What we do know is that come 29 April 2011 Kate will radiate beauty and elegance from head to toe. Her hair, her make-up and most importantly her dress will inspire a generation of bridal designers and brides around the world. And just like that Issa London blue engagement dress, dressmakers will be sewing together a replica garment the minute the blushing bride is revealed to the world and the designer of the original dress will be catapulted into the spotlight.

👑👑👑 *Tip* 👑👑👑

If you are getting married, you should have a trial run-through a week before the wedding. Get your hair and make-up done and try on your dress, shoes and jewellery to make sure everything is exactly how you want it to be. This will help eliminate any potential problems that might occur on your big day.

ROYAL GOWNS AND THEIR DESIGNERS

❀ Mette-Marit of Norway opted for home-grown talent and wore a beautiful dress by Norwegian designer Ove Harder Finseth.

❀ Like Mette-Marit, Mary of Denmark chose home-grown talent too and wed in a dress by Danish designer Uffe Frank.

❀ Valentino designed wedding gowns for both Princess Maxima of Netherlands and Crown Princess Marie-Chantal of Greece.

❀ Queen Elizabeth and her sister Princess Margaret both chose wedding gowns by British designer Norman Hartnell for their special occasion. Norman also dressed the Queen for another important landmark, her coronation.

- Bruce Oldfield, the man tipped to be Kate's designer, was the man behind Queen Rania of Jordan's gold-embroidered wedding gown.
- Letizia, Princess of Asturias got married in a Manuel Pertegaz design.
- Crown Princess Victoria of Sweden wore Swedish designer Par Engsheden creation.
- Grace Kelly's fairytale gown was created for her by MGM costume designer Helen Rose.
- Lady Diana's iconic dress was by Welsh designer David and Elizabeth Emmanuel and featured a twenty-five foot train and ten thousand hand-sewn pearls and sequins.

THE RING

If Kate follows royal tradition, and it is expected that she will, her wedding ring is likely to be made from a nugget of Welsh gold. Since the tradition was started by the Queen Mother in 1923, Welsh gold has been used for royal brides ever since. The Queen in 1947, Princess Margaret in 1960, the Princess Anne in 1973, Princess Diana in 1981 and Camilla in 2005 all had rings made from the same Welsh nugget. The Queen was presented with more Welsh gold after her original nugget, which had created many wonderful rings for the monarchy, ran out, so there will be plenty still in supply to create a wonderful gold band for Kate.

THE BOUQUET

Flowers have always played a crucial role in a royal wedding. From Diana's flamboyant bouquet containing gardenias, stephanotis, lily of the valley, freesias, golden Earl Mountbatten roses, odontoglossum orchids, plus myrtle, veronica, ivy and tradescantia to Camilla's dainty bouquet of grey and cream auriculas, lily of the valley and myrtle arrangement, there has been a whole range of different flowers used to create a truly royal bouquet. However, all royal wedding bouquets have included a sprig of myrtle to symbolise a happy marriage.

Kate is likely to follow the royal family tradition when it comes to the design of her bouquet and include a sprig of myrtle. The sprig of myrtle is taken from the bush grown from the original myrtle taken from Queen Victoria's wedding bouquet. There is also another royal tradition Kate is likely to follow, as she will place her bouquet on the Tomb of the Unknown Soldier at Westminster Abbey.

Traditions aside, the rest of the bouquet will be made up of flowers carefully selected by Kate. And although the style and shape of the bouquet will largely depend on the design and colour of Kate's dress, she is likely to pick seasonal flowers, like white lilies which are rumoured to be one of Kate's favourite flowers.

Whatever choice Kate makes it will be the right choice and will enhance the enchantment of the day.

♛ ♛ ♛ *Tip* ♛ ♛ ♛

SPRING WEDDING FLOWERS IN SEASON

Casa Blanca Lily
The Casa Blanca Lily means 'celebration' and is a very popular flower for wedding bouquets. The white lily is rumoured to be one of Kate's favourite flowers.

Daffodil
As William is Prince of Wales, there is a big possibility that a beautiful selection of narcissus or white daffodils will be included in the bouquet. The daffodil is the Welsh emblem.

Lily of the Valley
The beautiful Lily of the Valley is only in season during April and May and is one of the more expensive flowers. The small white flowers have a distinctive fragrance to invoke the senses. They also work well for men's buttonholes (boutonnieres).

Roses
Most bridal bouquets and arrangements include roses. Roses are ancient symbols of love and beauty. Rose means 'pink' or 'red' in a variety of languages.

Sweet Pea
Sweet peas are the wedding flowers par excellence. They are the most popular choice of flower for brides planning a spring or early summer wedding. They come in a variety of pastel colours including white, pink, coral and lavender.

Gerber Daisy
The Gerber Daisy is a useful flower that can easily harmonise colours within a bouquet of flowers especially tulips. It is also an excellent choice for brides who wish to make a statement as it adds dramatic colour.

Kate's bridal bouquet checklist

Bridal party and family
☑ Bouquet
☑ Pippa Middleton and bridesmaids' bouquets, and/or flowers for their hair
☑ Carole Middleton and Queen Elizabeth's corsages
☑ Prince William, Prince Harry, Prince Charles, and Michael Middleton and Prince Philip's boutonnieres

Ceremony Decorations
☑ Main altar
☑ Side arrangements
☑ Candelabra
☑ Candle flowers
☑ Pew decorations
☑ Guestbook table decorations
☑ Floral garland

Reception Decorations
☑ Top table arrangements
☑ Guest table centrepieces
☑ Table and chair accent flowers
☑ Cake table arrangement
☑ Gift table arrangement

THE HONEYMOON

Even the most modest of weddings is stressful and tiring to organise so imagine the pressures put upon William and Kate to deliver the wedding of century! They will both definitely need a private honeymoon to relax, unwind and celebrate being a married couple together.

Where will we find Kate and William?

Balmoral

For decades, Balmoral has offered peace and seclusion to royal honeymooners. No less than six newly-married royal couples have enjoyed honeymoons at Balmoral, including the Queen and Prince Philip. Scotland is very much a part of William and Kate's love story; after all, it is where they met. Kate adores the tranquillity that is found at Balmoral. It would be very surprising if they did not choose to spend at least a part of their honeymoon in Scotland.

Africa

William and Kate are already big fans of Africa – William proposed in Kenya, after all – and if they decided to go back to Africa they could expect to enjoy candle-lit dinners deep in the jungle, romantic walks on white powdery beaches, and champagne lunches looking out into the wilderness.

New Zealand

Prince William's first official foreign visit to Australia and New Zealand was a massive success and there has been a long tradition of new royal couples visiting the important Commonwealth countries as soon as possible, so the newly married couple could consider the islands of North Queensland for a secret romantic getaway.

Princess Catherine

Kate is already one of the most followed fashion-savvy royals in the world and is fast becoming a global fashion icon. With her love of boutique designers as well as high-street favourites, she has her very own unique and effortless fashion identity, which has and will continue to set the fashion scene alight.

Looking back at Kate's fashion transition over the years, it is clear that she has developed a strong style identity that is timeless as well as being true to her roots. She knows how to flatter her best features by choosing the correct silhouettes, colours and hats and she also knows how to disguise her flaws perfectly.

Although her style will continue to evolve as a member of the royal family and to accommodate royal protocol, one thing is for certain. Kate will continue to remain true to herself and she will no doubt always retain the girl-next-door quality that the world has embraced. Whereas Princess Diana became the couture darling of the world, Kate will be her own woman and will undoubtedly inspire a new generation of fashionistas with her effortlessly cool and conservatively chic image.

The world will be watching and waiting in anticipation for Catherine, Princess of Style to emerge, inspire and shine brightly as a 21st-century royal beacon of fashion.

STOCKISTS AND USEFUL WEBSITES

All About Coats
allaboutcoats.co.uk
0844 770 5838

Anya Hindmarch
anyahindmarch.com
020 7501 0177

Barbour
barbour.com
0191 455 4444

Bollé
bolle.com
+33 1 41 44 94 80

Bruce Oldfield
bruceoldfield.com
020 7584 1363

Burberry
burberry.com
customerservice@burberry.com

Chanel
chanel.com
Clogau Gold
clogau.co.uk
enquiries@clogau.co.uk

Coast
coast-stores.com

Cucinelli
brunellocucinelli.it

Ebay
ebay.co.uk

Elizabeth and David Emanuel
davidemanuel.com/couture
elizabethemanuel.co.uk
020 7289 4545

Florence and Fred
clothingattesco.com
08450 755 000

Harvey Nichols
harveynichols.com
0845 604 1888

Holly Fulton
hollyfulton.com
holly@hollyfulton.com

Hunter
hunter-boot.com
0131 240 3672

Issa London
issalondon.com
020 7352 4241

Jenny Packham
jennypackham.com
020 7428 4951

Jigsaw
jigsaw-online.com
020 8392 5603

Joules
joules.com
0845 250 7170

Katherine Hooker
katherinehooker.com
0207 352 5091

Kew
kew-online.com
020 8487 2000

Libélula
libelula-studio.com
07986 583 238
Links
linksoflondon.com
0844 477 0909

Lipsy
lipsy.co.uk
enquiries@lipsy.co.uk

Mango
mango.com
0845 082 2448

Manuel Pertegaz
pertegaz.es
+34 93 209 5922

Massimo Dutti
massimodutti.com

Matches
matchesfashion.com
0845 6025 612

Mulberry
mulberry.com
01761 234200

Neiman Marcus
neimanmarcus.com

Nordstrom
shop.nordstrom.com

Norman Hartnell
normanhartnell.com
020 7734 2436

Osman Yousefzada
osmanyousefzada.com
020 7724 9414

Pai Skincare
paiskincare.com
0208 994 4656

Philip Treacy
philiptreacy.co.uk

Prada
prada.com
+39 02 550281

QVC
qvcuk.com
0800 51 41 31

Reiss
reissonline.com
0845 604 7457

Richard Ward Salon
richardward.com
020 7730 1222

Schoffel
schoffel.co.uk
01572 770900

Stella McCartney
stellamccartney.co.uk
0203 4021 925

Temperley
temperleylondon.com
0207 229 7957

Tesco's Elevation Snow Range
clothingattesco.com
08450 755 000

The Natural Sapphire Company
thenaturalsapphirecompany.com
020 7043 3450

TK Maxx
tkmaxx.com
customerservice@tjxeurope.com

Topshop
topshop.com
customer.service@topshop.com

Turnbull & Asser
turnbullandasser.com
020 7808 3000

Uffe Frank
uffefrank.com
+39 338 248 1383

Ugg Boots
uggaustralia.com
0207 949 1114

Valentino
valentino.com

Vaseline
vaseline.com
0800 591720

Whistles
whistles.co.uk
0845 899 1222

William & Son
williamandson.com
020 7493 8385

Zara
zara.com
0800 030 4238

ACKNOWLEDGEMENTS

This book is dedicated to my mum and late father, without whose love, support and guidance I would not be where I am today. A big thank you to Chris and Adele for their patience and help and to the rest of my family for everything they do. Thanks to John Blake and the first-class John Blake team. I hope all the Kate fans out there enjoy reading the book as much as I enjoyed researching and writing it.

SOURCES

The research for this book was conducted using a wealth of sources including books, television programmes, websites, newspapers and magazines. Special thanks go to:

Hello!, the *Daily Mail*, the *Guardian*, the *Express*, the *Sun*, the *Mirror*, the *Independent*, *The Huffington Post*, *The Lazy Goddess*, *The Lazy Princess*, *William and Kate: The Love Story*, *Marie Claire*, *Grazia*, *Vogue*, BBC News, *Harper's Bazaar*, the *News of the World*, *Now*, the *Daily Telegraph*, *The Times*, Rex, Style Junkee, hangbag.com, Party Pieces, suite101.com, *Elle*, *Cosmopolitan*, Fashion for Nerds, www.alreadypretty.com, Channel 5 TV, www.royal.gov.uk, www.royalcourt.se, www.queenrania.jo, www.casareal.es, www.kongehuset.no, http://princess-prep.com.

PICTURE CREDITS